FOREWORD BY DR. DANIEL AMEN

ACCIDENTAL HYPNOSIS

EXPOSING THE HIDDEN INFLUENCES THAT
CONTROL YOUR MIND AND YOUR LIFE

LAURA B. TEMIN, LMFT, LPC

Copyright © 2022 by Laura B. Temin, LMFT, LPC

All rights reserved. No part of this book may be used or reproduced in any manner whatsoever without prior written consent of the authors, except as provided by the United States of America copyright law.

Published by Best Seller Publishing®, St. Augustine, FL
Best Seller Publishing® is a registered trademark
Printed in the United States of America.
ISBN: 978-1-956649-90-1

This publication is designed to provide accurate and authoritative information with regard to the subject matter covered. It is sold with the understanding that the publisher is not engaged in rendering legal, accounting, or other professional advice. If legal advice or other expert assistance is required, the services of a competent professional should be sought. The opinions expressed by the authors in this book are not endorsed by Best Seller Publishing® and are the sole responsibility of the author rendering the opinion.

For more information, please write:
Best Seller Publishing®
53 Marine Street
St. Augustine, FL 32084
or call 1 (626) 765-9750
Visit us online at: www.BestSellerPublishing.org

DEDICATION

This book is dedicated to:

All who walked through my doors—clients and students—for placing your trust in me. You taught me to listen on a deeper level and showed me where I could improve. Your faith in me fueled my determination to keep learning and growing. Thank you.

My Mentors who generously invested their time, energy, and love in me as I pursued my goals. Thank you.

My Husband, who is always supportive and whose belief in me made the publishing of this book possible. Thank you.

My Subconscious Mind. Thank you for revealing what needs to be seen and addressed. For showing me that even the difficulties can be stepping stones. And for steadfastly holding onto my dreams and goals, pushing me forward.

And to Every Person who reads this book. May this book add value to your life and provide answers you seek. Or perhaps inspire you to join me and become certified in hypnotherapy so that you, too, can enjoy a rewarding career, positively changing lives. Thank you.

TABLE OF CONTENTS

DEDICATION III
FOREWORD 1
INTRODUCTION 3
   Hindsight 3
   Hidden in Plain Sight 5

1 BELIEFS 7
   In the Blink of an Eye, Life-Altering Decisions Are Made! 15
   Our Beliefs Can Build or Destroy Relationships 18
   The Aha Moment 24

2 THE POWER OF SUGGESTION 27
   Suggestion and Its Connection to Belief 29
   The Power of Negative Self-Talk 33
   The Formation of Beliefs 45

3 HYPNOSIS 49
   Hypnosis, Trance, and Suggestion 52
   Spontaneous Accidental Self-Hypnosis 55
   Spontaneous Accidental Hypnosis and Illness 60

4 SABOTAGED 71
   Why the Cookies Win 74
   Suggestibility 81
   False Memories 84

5 REPETITION AND ASSOCIATION 87
   Learning, Advertising, and Laws of Hypnosis 89
   Conditioning 95
   Hypnotherapy 97

6 HIDDEN HYPNOSIS: ADVERTISING AND ALCOHOL 103
   Advertising — An Insidious Form of Accidental Hypnosis 107
   Alcohol 108
   Brainwave States 115
   Chasing a Memory of Fun — Addiction 118

7 HIDDEN HYPNOSIS: FOOD AND THE AMERICAN DREAM 125
   Targeting Youth 128
   The Temptation Train 132
   Partial Truth, Confusion, and Omission Strategy 134
   Addictive by Design 139
   Counter Sales and Add-On Sales 143

8 **HIDDEN HYPNOSIS: POLITICAL PERSUAsion.** 147
  Fear, Worry, Persuasion 150
  Strategies of Persuasion 161
  Self-Persuasion 167

9 **TRAUMA** 177
  Trauma Follows Drama 183
  Trauma and Hypnosis 189
  Setting the Stage — Parental Relationships 193

CONCLUSION 203
  Endings and New Beginnings 203
  A Dose of Prevention 214
  You Can't Keep a Good Dream Down 215

RESOURCES 219
  Personal Resources 219
  Professional Resources 219
  Programs and Seminars 220

THE LAWS OF HYPNOSIS 223

ENDNOTES 225

FOREWORD

While I was in medical school, I signed up for a monthlong elective in hypnosis, and it had a powerful impact on me. I put my training in medical hypnosis into action while I was interning in the emergency room at the Walter Reed Army Medical Center in Washington, DC. A patient named Beth, who had a blood clot that had caused her leg to swell, was getting prepped for surgery, and the medical team was trying to start an IV in her foot. But every time they touched her swollen foot, Beth let out a scream. With every poke of the needle, the poor woman screamed louder.

I hated seeing her suffer like this. I asked the internal medicine chief resident if I might try to start the IV. She glared at me condescendingly but said I could give it a try. I walked around the gurney to be near Beth's head and established eye contact with her. Then I asked her to slow her breathing. I then guided her into a hypnotic state that helped Beth feel more relaxed. Next, I asked her to imagine herself putting her feet in a pool of warm water, allowing her blood vessels to dilate. Almost immediately, a vein clearly appeared on her foot, and I gently slipped the needle into it—no screaming from Beth.

Since then, I have used medical hypnosis in my clinical psychiatric practice at Amen Clinics for over thirty years. I have found it to be a potent tool to enhance neuroplasticity that can help people so many ways, including with anxiety, depression, pain, fatigue, stress, tension headaches, stopping smoking, losing weight, and more.

That's why I'm so thrilled that my friend and colleague, Laura Temin, has written this wonderful book. In *Accidental Hypnosis*, Laura reveals the power of hypnosis in our lives. But she isn't writing about the kind of hypnosis that takes place in those stage shows in Las Vegas. What makes this book so compelling is that it shows how so much of our lives is influenced by an accidental form of hypnosis—one that is hidden in plain sight.

Most people don't have any idea that automatic thoughts and subconscious beliefs are driving our habitual behaviors. In this insightful, engaging, and fun-to-read book, Laura shows readers how to become more aware of these accidental hypnotic states and how to identify the triggers that spark them. Even better, she offers simple guidelines to use the most powerful elements of hypnosis to help you consciously regain control of your thoughts, actions, and life.

Daniel G. Amen, M.D.
Founder of Amen Clinics

INTRODUCTION

Hindsight

"If only …"

"I wish I could …"

"I don't understand why …"

Every one of us has unrealized dreams. Every one of us has a past. And every one of us desperately wishes to change certain aspects of ourselves, our situations, and our future. Yet no matter how hard we try, no matter how badly we want it, certain things seem out of reach or beyond our control. Why? What are we missing?

What if … what seems unattainable, impossible, or unresolvable really isn't? What if the real reason you can't break that habit, reach that goal, or solve that problem is completely different from what you and the experts believe? What if that is why your attempts have been unsuccessful?

Since hindsight is 20/20, I'm going to start with the bottom line first. Then we'll go back to the beginning and break down *how* our seemingly unsolvable problems really form, *why* certain goals seem out of reach, and *what* you need to know and understand in order to be in charge of your life.

I'm licensed as a Marriage and Family Therapist and a Professional Counselor. I earned my graduate degree in Counseling Psychology.

Yet the information I am about to share with you wasn't taught to me in graduate school. It wasn't taught to me in college. And it wasn't taught to me in grade school. My professors didn't discuss this information. My colleagues didn't discuss this information. In fact, none of the fully accredited colleges and universities of higher education taught this information.

How could it be that no one was teaching information that could prevent people from being victimized by debilitating problems, especially problems that are avoidable and resolvable? How could it be that people far more knowledgeable than I am did not discuss this information or insist that it be part of every educational system? Surely I was not the only person to recognize its life-altering power. Was it misunderstood? Or was it simply hidden in plain sight?

Hidden in Plain Sight

Imagine what it would be like if, for almost a year, you were plagued by nightmares that were so vivid and so scary that you punched and kicked your spouse in your sleep, thinking they were "the bad guy." Of course, you tried to fix this problem. You saw the doctor. You took sleep aids. You did everything you could. But nothing worked. And then suddenly, within just a few weeks, you were peacefully sleeping through the night. How? Because someone understood something that had previously been overlooked.

Imagine being saddled with an addiction for over 40 years and unable to break free. You were controlled by relentless cravings day and night, and despite your best attempts to free yourself, you continuously lost the battle. And then, suddenly, within just a few days to a few weeks—poof! The cravings were gone. How? Because someone understood something that had previously been misunderstood.

And imagine how you would feel if your spouse had had an affair 10 years earlier but you could not stop replaying certain scenarios over and over in your mind. And each time you drove down a certain block, you smelled a certain scent, or each time your call to your spouse went to voicemail, you felt anxious and panicky. Of course you went for counseling. Of course you tried to forget the past, but you were constantly haunted by the memories. And then suddenly, within just a few months, you felt a sense of peace, even in those previously triggering situations. How? Because someone understood something that others missed.

Over the last 23 years, I've had the privilege of sitting with people like these who had spent countless years talking to doctors, therapists, and professionals in every field. And although the clinicians provided value, the problem persisted. Their struggles to break free from addictions and habits, to make peace with the past, to override traumas, to dissolve anger, to strengthen relationships, to get unstuck, and to feel better, were met with limited success. Yet, over and over again, I found that the solution to these problems and others remained hidden in plain sight.

What I discovered was as eye-opening and life-changing for me as it was for my clients. *And I am about to share everything I learned with you so you can reclaim your life.*

For those of you who are in helping professions, I hope this information sparks your interest in hypnotherapy. Dr. Oz recently told me how much he valued hypnotherapy and was surprised that it remains such an overlooked approach in medicine and mental health.

1

BELIEFS

Life is about believing.
—Evander Holyfield

Evander Holyfield, four-time heavyweight champion of the world (shown here with me), said: "When I was eight years old, my coach told me, 'You can be the heavyweight champion of the world.' I said, 'But I'm only eight years old.' He said, 'You won't always be eight.'" Evander stopped for a moment and said, "When my coach told me that, I believed him (because next week I was going to be nine)." And he looked at me and said, "Life is about believing." Evander told his coach, "I have to ask my mama. And if my mama says I can, then I can." After a conversation with his coach, his mother told him, yes, he could. And he believed her. And that sealed the deal. And the rest is history.

That is the power of belief. And belief is where it all begins. As you read this book, you will come to recognize the role conscious and subconscious beliefs have in our lives. You will recognize that many of the celebrities whose stories I share have one thing in common. They tap in to the power of their mind and use it with intention and purpose—even though many of them might never realize they are accessing the subconscious mind or the power of hypnosis.

ACCIDENTAL HYPNOSIS

Michael grew up in a family in which it was normal to enjoy a beer or two or three, or some wine at the end of the day, and certainly on the weekend. Ball games were always accompanied by burgers and a beer, even if they were watched at home. His family loved to entertain, and there was nothing more important than good old southern hospitality. Friends, family, and friends of friends were always dropping by. Their home was the gathering place. You often heard Michael's mom say, "It's downright rude not to have food for your guests. And everyone loves to snack." Their fridge and pantry were well stocked with cookies, pastries, chips, dips, hoagies, and cheese sticks. And, of course, plenty of sodas, beer, and wine to wash it down with "because you never know when folks will drop by."

Mandy grew up in a family where organic foods were the norm. No GMO or processed foods were welcome. They made chickpea salads with avocado instead of mayonnaise. And cauliflower mash replaced pre-packaged white potatoes. Their dehydrator was their "healthy" snack machine, which turned beets into pretty red beet chips.

Mandy was taught to check the labels and ingredients in anything she considered putting in her mouth because "you are what you eat" and "dead, packaged foods have dangerous ingredients which make people sick over time." Mandy loved making almond milk with her mom and using the almond flour to make coconut pie for her sleepover parties.

You can see that Mandy and Michael had very different backgrounds and received very different messages growing up.

Michael met Mandy during their freshman year at college. Michael invited her out on a date. He knew she liked nature, so he suggested a picnic and he told her to leave everything up to him, that he would prepare a picnic feast. On their special date, he packed a beautiful picnic basket filled with white embossed napkins, colorful plastic wine glasses, hoagies, beer, wine, and desserts. He chose all the foods that people love, because he wanted to make sure she felt special. They were both excited to spend the day together. They laughed and chatted all the way up to the picnic grounds.

What do you think happened when he opened the picnic basket? The mood changed drastically. Mandy was surprised and extremely disappointed. She felt insulted. Her *interpretation* was that he was "lazy and disrespectful" because "he threw the worst-quality, highly processed foods and poisonous drinks into a basket." To her, it was obvious that he didn't care very much about her. To her, his actions proved that he didn't think she was worth his time. When she came home that day, she told her friends, "I would never do that to anyone, especially someone I care about."

She never said a word about the food or her feelings to Michael because she had been told, "If you don't have something nice to say, don't say anything." But her face and attitude said it all.

Michael was waiting for a big smile, a big hug, and a big thank you. But it never came. He was hurt and surprised. After all, he worked extra shifts to earn the money to pay for this feast. He even passed up family gatherings so he could work extra shifts. On top of that, he burned gas driving all around town to get specialty meats at the best prices. He had bought everything that he knew people loved, because he'd wanted to make it special for Mandy.

In the blink of an eye, Mike's impression of Mandy changed. He saw her as "downright rude and insensitive." She was "a b****." And suddenly she reminded him of his cousin's ex-wife who was never happy with anything his cousin did. He remembered that his cousin had spent years trying to please his ex-wife but she was never happy. Mike came to the conclusion that Mandy was just like her. Mike vowed that he would never waste his money on a girl again until she proved she was worth it. He told his friends, "The next time I go out with a new girl, she can meet me at the college cafeteria and buy her own lunch!"

It's easy to see how Mike's and Mandy's different upbringings dictated their values, their expectations, and influenced their interpretations about one another. Can you see how quickly their beliefs formed? And how feelings and interpretations appear to be facts? Can you see how much power our interpretations and misinterpretations have over us?

> Our beliefs influence our thoughts, feelings, and behavior, yet we remain blind to the process.

Mike and Mandy are not much different from you and me. The details may be different, but we are all influenced by our interpretations and we don't even realize it.

It almost doesn't matter what a person struggles against. It could be weight, goals, confidence, addiction, finances, relationships, or anything else. In the final analysis, practically everything is influenced by this one shared element: ***What We Believe***. Our beliefs influence our thoughts, feelings, and behavior, and they ultimately direct the course of our lives. Yet, we remain blind to the entire process.

This is what I've noticed about beliefs:

- Most of us consider our beliefs to be facts, simply because we believe them
- Our beliefs are so enmeshed into the fiber of who we are that we barely notice them or the power they have over us
- Over time our beliefs become so much a part of us that we don't stop to consider where they came from or their validity in the present moment

- What we stand for, what we are willing to fight for, and how we live are based on our beliefs

This process is so deeply embedded in our everyday thinking that it is easy to miss. *It's hidden in plain sight.*

We make assumptions about people based on how we would behave if *we* were in their situation. For example, if I would never yell at my dog but if my new friend yells at her dog, I might believe that she isn't the nice person I thought she was. I might believe that I could never trust her to pet-sit. Or I might believe that she is an angry person or an impatient person. If someone I once dated yelled at their dog, and they turned out to be an angry person, I might automatically be reminded of him and unintentionally attribute his angry disposition to my new friend. On the other hand, I might simply believe that she is just having a bad day.

- Our interpretations feed our beliefs
- Our beliefs dictate our behavior
- Our beliefs have the power to change the course of our lives

Mandy interpreted Michael's choice of picnic foods to mean that he was lazy and did not care. Why? Because her mother taught her that processed foods are bad for you and that healthy foods equal love. Michael said he'd take care of everything, but she didn't feel taken care of by his choices. Her interpretation was automatic. As thinking humans, we automatically assign a meaning to behavior. Meanings help us make sense of our world. It's natural, but if we don't realize that we are the ones giving meaning to the behavior or that our interpretations may be inaccurate, it will cost us dearly.

We can only know what we know. We're each limited by our own three-pound brain. Our brain interprets the world through our own experiences, our own eyes, and our own ears. That's why it never occurred to Mandy that Michael truly did care and did live up to his word. She misinterpreted his actions and catalogued that misinterpretation as a fact, which in turn created her new beliefs about him.

Michael was also making meaning from this experience through his own three-pound brain and through his own eyes, ears, and experiences up to this point in his life. Because Michael invested emotionally and sacrificed more time, energy, and money to make their picnic special, his reaction was more severe.

- Michael associated the negative qualities belonging to his cousin's ex-wife to Mandy, deciding she was "just like his cousin's ex."
- He made the assumption that since his cousin's ex-wife was never happy, Mandy too, would never be happy. (This is the Law of Association, and I will come back to this later.)

- As a result, he decided he would *never allow himself to be taken advantage of again.*
- And in that moment, he took this vow: Never to spend money on a woman again until she proved she was worth it.

IN THE BLINK OF AN EYE, LIFE-ALTERING DECISIONS ARE MADE!

The mind interprets other people's behavior based on what that behavior would mean if they, themselves, behaved that way. The mind pays attention to negative feelings and seeks to protect itself. And the mind draws conclusions from our interpretations.

These conclusions have the potential to dictate how we move through life. We don't realize this is happening and we become victims of our own minds. We rarely stop to evaluate because we confuse our feelings with facts, and we are completely blind to this process.

Michael's *interpretation* of Mandy's behavior profoundly influenced his thoughts and his actions. It became a *generalized belief,* meaning he attributed this experience to all interactions with women. And then it became a vow, *a decision that dictated all future actions.*

Michael's decision "not to waste money on a girl again" was carried all the way into his adult life. He tested his dates before opening his heart or his wallet. *That one experience completely shifted the way he thought about dating and women.* He went from being emotionally open and generous to being suspicious. His experience with Mandy and his interpretation of the experience made him cautious, untrusting, and self-protective. All of these significant shifts in his beliefs happened very quickly in response to this one emotionally charged experience. And it altered the way he thought about women for decades.

Our beliefs are internal but are also projected back into the world.

Over and over again, in my counseling practice, as people shared their stories, I saw that it could take as little as one emotionally charged situation to completely change the course of a person's life. Can you imagine how different Michael's life might have been if he understood this concept?

ACCIDENTAL HYPNOSIS

These on-the-spot interpretations are typical for all of us. But when we're in the moment, we don't realize what's happening. We don't understand how important it is to pull back and question our beliefs. It's our inability to see the forest for the trees in the moment that causes us to misjudge without question. That's a major contributor to solidifying these powerful beliefs in the mind.

Why does it happen so fast? Because highly charged emotions trigger our survival response.

The subconscious mind feels the pain and says, "I never want to be in this situation again. I can't let anyone hurt me this way again!" It puts a *"Stop" marker* in place to avoid future problems. Once the decision is made, it's locked in place. And it remains a steadfast commitment (until it's recognized and dissolved by someone who understands the influence of the subconscious mind and knows how to resolve it). But too many people don't realize they're victims of their own mind, and too many clinicians confuse the symptom with the problem. Not because they're trying to keep a person in therapy forever, but because traditional psychology programs barely address the subconscious mind. It's misunderstood and overlooked.

In summary, the mind gives meaning to every experience.

- The meaning/interpretation we come away with is translated into a belief about us, others, or the world around us.

- Eventually those beliefs become the foundation of how we operate in the world and what we expect from others.

We live our lives based on the interpretations that we've accepted as true without discernment in that moment and without considering that we might be wrong. Once we accept our interpretations as true, we rarely question them. With time, those interpretations become incorporated into beliefs that influence how we feel about ourselves and our world. And we live our lives as *if* our beliefs are truth!

Our Beliefs Can Build or Destroy Relationships

One reason there are so many divorces and so many relationship problems is because, to some degree, we're under the impression that our partner holds the same values and expectations that we hold. In general, people automatically assume "My way is the normal way, and that's the way things should be." This assumption colors our expectations of our partner. Logically, we know people are different. But when we're caught off guard by differences, the emotional mind overrides the logical mind. Think about your own relationship or relationships you've seen.

When our partner behaves outside of our expectations, we frequently judge or assert blame. We see him or her as flawed or intentionally misbehaving.

ACCIDENTAL HYPNOSIS

Sheila's dad always put the seat down after he used the toilet. But Sheila's husband leaves the seat up. Sheila feels angry when she goes into the bathroom and the toilet seat is up. Her mind gives meaning to that behavior. Her automatic internal response is, *"You know you're supposed to put the seat down. That's the right way. That's what men do when they care."* Then her mind follows it with *"Since everyone knows that, it's obvious that if you leave the seat up, it's intentional."* And the "logical" conclusion Sheila comes to is that her husband is *purposely being inconsiderate*, which leads her to believe *he is selfish*, or *he does not care*, or ... (fill in the blank).

Leaving the seat up becomes *evidence and proof* that her husband doesn't care about or love her. Sheila uses the toilet several times a day, every day. And every time she sees that toilet seat up, she's reminded that her husband doesn't care about her or that he's selfish. That message is reinforced multiple times a day. This reinforcement strengthens the message and her negative feelings.

How do you think Sheila feels toward her husband when she believes her husband doesn't care or is selfish? How do you think she treats him when she doesn't feel loved or respected? She's probably short-tempered and distant rather than loving and kind. But her husband has no idea *why* she's acting so cold. And *he makes his own set of interpretations*, which lead to his own set of behaviors that also impact their relationship.

19

Back to Sheila. Once the premise is accepted, the mind looks for evidence *everywhere* to prove that her husband is inconsiderate or doesn't love her or whatever conclusion her mind established. This happens automatically because the initial belief that she is loved or cared for is now in question.

> Past traumatic events make people hyper-vigilant. As a result, their mind magnifies every inconsistency.

The mind wants to feel safe and comfortable. If we see signs that indicate we're not loved in our marriage, we feel uneasy or vulnerable. If Sheila was mistreated in a previous relationship or witnessed physical or emotional abuse, it could easily trigger the survival response. Past traumatic events make people hypervigilant. And as a result, their mind magnifies every inconsistency. It's like a missile that is programmed to hit a target. When we experience trauma or volatility in a relationship, the subconscious mind notices everything that is similar, so we can protect ourselves.

This is why any time Sheila sees the toilet seat up, it subconsciously tells her that she is not safe. She may not actually think, "I am not safe." She may not even know she does not feel safe. She just knows that she is feeling distressed, uncomfortable, unimportant, or unloved.

Most people don't question their beliefs. Our beliefs are woven into the fiber of our being. We become blind to the control they have over us, even though they pop up throughout the day. Yet we continue to respond to the world based on our beliefs.

Dr. John Gottman, relationship expert, tells us that couples essentially sweep their upsets under the rug for three to seven years before seeking marriage counseling. As a licensed Marriage Therapist, I know that to be true. When couples come for counseling, they confuse the real problem with the symptoms of the problem because they don't realize what's really going on, or why. They just know that they can't talk to each other without one of them arguing or shutting down. They attribute negative character traits to their partner/spouse and they don't realize that their assumptions are based on their own interpretations, not facts.

What if Sheila's husband's father always left the toilet seat up, and that was normal in his household? What if Sheila's husband had no idea that she has a completely different interpretation of the toilet seat being up or down? What if he had no idea that there could be a different set of standards and expectations around toilet seats?

Sheila gives meaning to his actions, based on her history. Her interpretations form beliefs about her husband and their relationship. And because she thinks that her way of thinking is normal for everyone, her interpretation is seen as evidence. Because it would be true of her, if she did it. Those beliefs work behind the scenes against their relationship.

Let's take it one step further. If she believes her husband is selfish, then her mind will look for evidence that he is selfish. If she believes he doesn't care, her mind will look for evidence that he doesn't care. And, of course, she will react to her beliefs and treat him differently based on her beliefs.

Unchecked Beliefs Undermine Relationships, and It Happens Beneath the Level of Awareness

That's what happened with Michael. He made a decision based on his interpretation of Mandy's behavior. He decided that he was never going to be taken advantage of, or place himself in a position to be hurt, again. This belief dictated his behavior all the way into his 40s in that he refused to take a woman out for anything more than coffee until she had "proved" that she was worth it.

He was so hurt by the incident that his subconscious mind held on to that experience. Every time he considered dating, his mind automatically recalled the incident and the feeling associated with the incident, which put him into a cautious mode. His mind triggered the subconscious thought, *WAIT! Not so fast. You can be hurt. You need to be careful.* He may not even have recognized that that's what he was thinking. Most people don't. He's was just thinking that he needed to be careful. Or he may just have felt uncomfortable, hesitant, or conflicted for a moment. And then his automatic knee-jerk response was to protect himself.

Michael wants to find love, but this knee-jerk response gets in the way. Think about people you know who are continually struggling with dating or with relationships. Think about what you know of their history. Often, there's an emotional experience that created a belief, and it is that belief that's carried into their current situation. And that is what's working against them. It may not even be from their own personal experience. They might have witnessed a painful experience with a parent, relative, or loved one. Interpretations and decisions are made in any given moment and can be carried forward for a lifetime.

TIP: Sometimes patterns are an indication that there are underlying beliefs that are holding you hostage. If you're having problems in your relationship or with relationships in general, you might want to question whether patterns are plaguing you. **Take the free quiz** at: www.LauraTemin.com/patterns

If you're a clinician and interested in learning how to help couples build better relationships, release the trauma of betrayals, and understand more about the subconscious mind, you might be interested in our Hypnotherapy Certification Programs. Reach us at: www.hypnotherapy.School

The Aha Moment

What I saw over and over again was that underneath the client's seemingly unresolvable problems or unattainable goals were *beliefs*. And those beliefs were caused by their own interpretations and suggestions, or perhaps those of another person.

Those suggestions could be intentional or unintentional. Either way, they were extremely powerful. Why? Because suggestions are strengthened through repetition. And if a person is feeling overwhelmed or emotionally distressed at the time of the suggestion, that suggestion has even more power. When we're distressed or overwhelmed, suggestions and interpretations aren't properly questioned or well analyzed. As a result, that suggestion slips right into the mind as if it were a fact.

That's when I finally understood that what I was witnessing was the power of suggestion and accidental hypnosis.

Accidental Hypnosis: People think hypnosis is something a hypnotist does to them on a stage, but what I was witnessing was hidden in plain sight and far more powerful. I could see how this accidental form of hypnosis was hijacking a person's life, and yet they remained completely unaware. I came to understand that when a problem was not resolvable, despite how desperately a person wanted resolution and despite how hard they tried, it was frequently tied to a belief, and their subconscious mind was trying to protect them. In that aha moment, I realized why all their attempts to solve it had failed. Logic alone would never be able to fix the problem.

In the next few chapters, I will explain what hypnosis *really* is and how the power of suggestion works. Once you put these pieces together in your mind, you will hold the missing piece of the puzzle. You will see how interpretations create beliefs and how beliefs have the power to control lives. And you'll understand what you can do to take the power back in your own life.

2
THE POWER OF SUGGESTION

Fill your mind with faith, not fear.
—Dog the Bounty Hunter

Dog the Bounty Hunter, seen here with me, has undoubtedly mastered the power of suggestion. How many people do you know who confidently take on dangerous enemies without the protection of a gun? How does he manage the fear? He fills his mind with messages of faith and scripture rather than focusing on the voice of fear.

We had a conversation, and I asked him what he did to keep going in difficult situations. The more I listened to what Dog said, the more I realized that he was regularly flooding his mind with positive, powerful suggestions, not only in the face of fear but in regard to the important areas of life.

As you read this chapter, think about the kinds of suggestions you give yourself throughout the day. See if you can catch yourself in the midst of them. Notice if there is a theme to your self-talk when you're fearful, or when things are going your way.

Suggestion and Its Connection to Belief

We're always giving and receiving suggestions. Suggestions come from our bodies, our minds, from others, from events (as we saw with Michael and Mandy), and from the outside world.

Hunger

This illustration is labeled *Hunger*[1]. If you didn't know that, you might see the boy holding his stomach and *interpret* his facial expression, his body language, and the lightning-shaped lines around his stomach to mean that he has a stomachache because he ate all those foods in the bubble. If you noticed the word "Hunger" under the image, you might *interpret* the picture to mean that he is hungry and daydreaming about the food in the bubble.

If you knew that this boy was hungry and you offered him a fresh green salad instead of the food in the bubble, he might say to himself, "WHAT???? A salad??!!! That's bird food. I'm hungry. I want real food (the food in my mind/bubble)!"

If he were on a diet and felt deprived because he was avoiding sweets, he might be tasting that cupcake in his mind. Depending on what he tells himself, he will either talk himself into eating the cupcake or talk himself out of eating it. That's an example of the power of suggestion. Our self-talk and self-suggestions are ongoing in our minds. They run behind the scenes and beneath our awareness, yet they are continually influencing our feelings and controlling our behavior.

What exactly is the power of suggestion? Merriam-Webster.com defines *suggestion* this way:

- The process by which a physical or mental state is influenced by a thought or idea
- The process by which one thought leads to another, especially through association of ideas
- A slight indication or trace

All day long, and for as long as we are awake, the mind is actively evaluating and commenting on our current experiences and the events of the day. We talk to ourselves. We review what we heard from others. We review our accomplishments, our mistakes, and the emotionally impactful details.

> If we don't understand the power of suggestion, we can fall victim to our own fears or the influence of others.

If we're upset with ourselves, we might tell ourselves, "What an idiot I am. I can't believe I made such a silly mistake. They must think I'm a jerk. It will probably cost me that promotion/job/raise." Or we might tell ourselves, "It's not a life-or-death mistake, and I can take care of it quickly and put things right." Those are examples of suggestions we give ourselves. But we also receive suggestions from others.

Consider this scenario with John, a 50-year-old employee in the pool chemical distribution business. John's responsible for calculating how much product the company needs to keep in stock in order to meet their customers' seasonal demands. John gravely underestimated their upcoming needs. He hadn't anticipated that the pandemic would last. He didn't anticipate shortages of workers or increased gasoline prices.

Once his boss saw that demand was high and their supply was low, he called John into the office and questioned him. Later, John discussed the situation with a co-worker who said, *"That mistake is the beginning of the end. That's how companies get rid of people over 40. It happened to my uncle. Now it's happening to you. They'll build a case against you and track everything you do so they can fire you. You'd better start looking for a job."* Not only did John have his own fear messages running wild in his mind, but his co-worker also added the power of suggestion based on her own fears, history, and perspective.

When John returned home that evening, his wife hugged him and told him, "Everything happens for a reason. You've been a loyal employee, and with your years of experience and your dedication, anyone would be lucky to have you. Remember, sweetheart, there's a shortage of workers these days, so your new employer will give you a raise!"

Can you see how messages can be helpful and supportive and move us in positive ways, or scary and undermining and negatively impact or limit us? If we don't understand the power of suggestion, we might fall victim to our own fears or the opinions of others.

> **TIP:** The mind continually processes and sorts through each situation, making interpretations and attempting to make sense of it. Our internal chatter runs constantly. It becomes background noise in the mind, so we barely notice that we're conversing with ourselves. You'd be surprised at

what you could learn about yourself if you were to act as an observer of the chatter in your head.

It's helpful to write down your waking thoughts in the morning and track the repetitive thoughts you carry throughout the day. Most people have the same theme day after day. If your thoughts are fearful, anxious, or negative, simply take note of them. If they are negative, avoid judging yourself. You can't change what you're not aware of. And your only job with this is to understand your starting point so you can redirect yourself.

The Power of Negative Self-Talk

One thing worth knowing is that the subconscious mind always tries to protect us. It does this by triggering memories to help us avoid situations like those that have hurt us in the past. Research tells us that the mind is wired to pay attention to bad things over good things for survival. Its true purpose is to help us.

Does it surprise you that most people believe their negative self-talk over their positive self-talk? It's true! We all know smart, kind, good people who regularly put themselves down and are focused on every mistake and failure they make. Through the habit of repeating those scenarios in the mind and linking those negative experiences with the self, we accidentally strengthen the negative connection in the mind. You already know that once the mind accepts your interpretation or someone else's suggestion as a fact, it's on its way to becoming a belief.

You also know that when emotions are high, our feelings (which we perceive as facts) often override our logical thinking. Our analyzing ability simply takes a back seat to our emotions, and our emotions drive us. This is why intelligent, talented, caring people completely discount, negate, dismiss, and invalidate any evidence pointing to their successes and accomplishments. Instead, they stack the deck against themselves by recalling and magnifying every mistake they ever made. It doesn't matter what they've accomplished; they cannot allow themselves to believe it.

Our negative beliefs about ourselves accidentally become conditioned through repetition. Over time, we believe our negative self-talk and remain blind to our unintentional participation in the process.

Here's how it works:

- We continuously relive our past upsets, distressing incidents, and the blame and judgment from others
- We internalize those feelings, which strengthens those beliefs
- Eventually, we come to see those experiences as proof that we are horrible, stupid, (fill in the blank)

- We find it difficult to believe anything positive to the contrary

By tapping into *only* the unpleasant feelings and revisiting those situations and feelings, we unintentionally convince ourselves that we are defective, or less than, or even pathetic (or whatever the self-talk or judgment from others implied).

This unintentional reinforcement keeps us stuck in a negative loop and solidifies negative beliefs.

Imposter Syndrome

Psychology Today defines Imposter Syndrome in this way:

> *People who struggle with imposter syndrome believe that they are undeserving of their achievements and the high esteem in which they are, in fact, generally held. They feel that they aren't as competent or intelligent as others might think—and that soon enough, people will discover the truth about them. Those with imposter syndrome are often well accomplished; they may hold high office or have numerous academic degrees.*[2]

Can you see how imposter syndrome is feeling-driven? It's tied into the belief that you have to know everything, and if you don't you're a fraud. It's strengthened by revisiting every failure through emotional rehearsals.

Pete came from a hard-working lower-middle-class family. He had dyslexia and did poorly in school. Pete was told he was stupid and lazy because no one understood dyslexia or ADHD at that time. He didn't know that he was seeing letters backward, so he couldn't explain it. Of course, he was frustrated. He couldn't keep up with his classes and he had trouble focusing. He barely finished high school.

The message he heard over and over from his teachers and parents was that he was stupid. That he didn't measure up. That he would never amount to anything. Pete found a job as a bagger in the supermarket. His boss dabbled in the stock market, and that intrigued Pete. He asked his boss to teach him how to make money. Pete had an uncanny ability to understand financial concepts and a natural ability to analyze information and problem solve.

> **By tapping into only the unpleasant feelings and negative experiences, we unintentionally convince ourselves that we are defective.**

Today Pete owns a global securities firm with multiple locations around the world. He is often referred to as *brilliant*. He's extremely successful and is regularly asked to speak to audiences about the economy and current trends. Just the thought of speaking onstage brings up feelings of inadequacy and the fear that he might not know everything he needs to know and then people will see that he is stupid.

Is Pete an imposter? Is Pete stupid? Absolutely not! He's truly an expert in his field, but even an expert can't know everything. And being an expert in one area doesn't erase all of our insecurities. Despite all of his success, tucked away in his subconscious mind is the conditioned belief that he is stupid.

This is an example of the power of suggestion and what I am calling "Accidental Hypnosis." All the logic and evidence in the world doesn't eradicate beliefs held by the subconscious mind.

You're not an imposter. Like Pete, all of us are stuck in a loop of Accidental Self-Hypnosis.

To Recap:

- There's an event or experience that makes us feel insecure
- We're embarrassed, upset, or troubled by it
- The subconscious mind attempts to protect us
- We connect the upset with a self-diminishing statement
- The negative self-talk message is received as a fact and becomes a repeated suggestion to ourselves

- Thinking about the upset pulls up the matching distressing emotions such as insecurity, depression, anxiety, self-doubt, or fear
- Each time we relive it we reinforce the negative feelings and strengthen the negative statements
- The mind automatically recalls similar experiences from the past and, instead of realizing that we are meant to learn from it, it's interpreted as evidence that our negative self-assessment is true
- We intently focus on the negatives, and disregard and diminish the value of the positives
- The self-talk suggestions take on a life of their own
- Our thoughts trigger matching chemicals throughout the mind-body system
- Because we don't understand what's going on, we can't put it in perspective or stop it

That's how powerful suggestions can be. And how they root in the subconscious mind.

Zelda's Story

Zelda's parents were born in a country where boys had more freedom than girls, and the man was considered the head of the household. Young women were expected to marry and have a family of their own and care for their aging parents as well as their husband's aging parents.

ACCIDENTAL HYPNOSIS

Young men were expected to go to school and out into the world and eventually become successful businessmen. Zelda was the oldest of five children. Her father was short-tempered and demanding. He spoke down to her mother and to her. But he spoke differently to her brothers. Her brothers copied their father's behavior and spoke to Zelda the same way that her father spoke to her.

The way our parents behave is a form of suggestion. It's often an implied, indirect suggestion. They're modeling behavior for us, and we learn by watching and listening. Naturally, Zelda and her brothers saw and heard the differences.

The words Zelda often heard were, "Go now and take care of what your brother needs." What Zelda heard when her father made those statements was an *implied suggestion*. Her mind *interpreted* that command to mean that her needs didn't matter, that only her brother's needs mattered. Therefore, she didn't matter. And she was there to serve.

Young children don't understand the influence of culture. Even adults have difficulty making distinctions among cultural expectations, family expectations, parental expectations, individual expectations, realistic expectations, unrealistic expectations, and the influence of mental illness on expectations. Children don't have a category in their mind for mental health issues. They are scared when a parent is emotionally explosive, inconsistent, obnoxiously drunk, or out of control. But they can't fully distinguish between realistic and unrealistic expectations.

Children notice inconsistencies in behavior and in treatment. They recognize what is fair and what isn't. And they quickly see there are rules (whether or not they choose to follow them).

Children don't develop the ability to analyze until they are between the ages of 8 and 12. When they are young, they're still developing critical thinking. That puts them in a precarious situation because if they cannot fully analyze, and if they don't have a wide assortment of experiences to evaluate from, it's easy to misread and misunderstand. Because of that, their decisions are based only on what they see, hear, and feel at that moment or in the accumulated moments.

> If we can't resolve our primary relationship with our birth family, we're inclined to carry that experience and the patterns forward.

Children don't know that they lack all the necessary information. Even adults are often unaware that they may not have all the information they need or that they may be misreading a situation. When we're young, we, we also have magical thinking. If we hold bad thoughts about someone and something bad happens, we believe we are responsible.

Zelda yearned for love and attention. She *felt like* she could never please her father or her brothers no matter how hard she tried. Because of the way her father and brothers spoke to her and treated her, she determined she was unlovable. (Remember, feelings are perceived as facts.) She *felt like* there was something wrong with her. That was the way Zelda's young, inexperienced mind *interpreted* the words and her experiences. It's easy to see how and why she could come to believe "I am not loveable; I am not important. My feelings don't matter. There's something wrong with me."

What we see and experience growing up becomes normalized and familiar to us. We call these familiar experiences *knowns*. People tend to choose *knowns* over *unknowns* because they're familiar. They know what to expect with *knowns* but they have no reference point for *unknowns*, so the *unknowns* seem scarier. That's why people stay in jobs, careers, and relationships that aren't good for them— because they are *knowns*. You've heard the expression, "The devil you know is better than the devil you don't know." It refers to *knowns* and *unknowns*.

Zelda's beliefs resulted from those implied suggestions that her father modeled, which he never intentionally said or meant. I'm sure if he knew how she was interpreting his behaviors, he would have quickly addressed it and told her how much he loved and valued her. He would have told her that she was loveable and precious to him. But he could not read her mind and he was unaware that his cultural beliefs, which were intended to make her a good wife, were misunderstood. Surely he didn't want his daughter to believe she was unlovable. Surely he didn't think that there was something wrong with her. He was simply behaving in accordance with his culture and driven by his moods. Perhaps he had an anger problem, or maybe he was simply frustrated because he worked long hours and didn't earn the amount of money he wanted to earn.

But children don't know or understand what parents are going through. They don't know their parents' history, so they can only make sense of what they can see and understand in the moment. Children, as well as adults, infer meaning from what is seen and heard. Remember, we make judgments based on our feelings and believe them to be facts. And as you already know, our interpretations create our beliefs, and our beliefs influence our choices and behavior.

If we can't resolve our primary relationship with our birth family, we're inclined to carry that experience and the patterns forward. Our unfinished business travels forward with us and is acted out, to some degree, in our love relationships, and to some degree in all of our relationships.

Blind Spots

I began to see this pattern emerging with almost everyone who came through my door. I wondered how could it be that I was able to see these patterns but they weren't? The answer is Blind Spots.

Let's say you're driving and you want to change lanes. You look in the rear-view and side-view mirrors. The coast is clear. As you begin to move over, you catch a glimpse of a car that was there all the time but was invisible to you because it was hidden in your blind spot.

The more I listened to my clients, the more apparent it became to me that *we* act from within our blind spots. When things are in our blind spot, we can't see them. We don't know they are there. We don't recognize that we are being influenced. We certainly can't put things in perspective if we don't have all the information. And we don't understand what's happening or its impact on us. This happens to all of us because all of us have blind spots. We just don't know it. This sets us up as victims of our own thoughts, misinterpretations, self-talk, and intentional or unintentional suggestions from others. We're controlled by our own minds and we are blind to it. We believe that things are out of control. We don't think we're out of control or there's a problem with our way of thinking because our experiences and beliefs are woven into the fiber of who we are. And we don't realize what's happening.

In a nutshell:

- We frequently misinterpret the intended meaning of what we see and hear
- We underestimate the extent and impact on our lives
- We internalize the undermining, inaccurate messages
- Those messages begin to define how we see ourselves and the world
- Those negative, limiting suggestions become beliefs that control our lives

You cannot fix what you can't see and don't understand. That's why so many people never outgrow certain problems, no matter how hard they try or how much they want things to be different. The problem is seemingly unsolvable.

That's why it is so important that you understand how beliefs form AND the relationship between suggestion, interpretation, belief, and your subconscious mind. Our core beliefs can last a lifetime. They're woven into the fabric of our being. They touch every area of our lives.

Remember ... beliefs are powerful. Once you believe something, you no longer question its validity. If you don't question your beliefs, you're stuck in a holding pattern.

People are committed to their beliefs. Wars are fought based on beliefs. Our religious and political beliefs and our beliefs about life, health, freedom, and justice are some of our most strongly held beliefs. You can see it throughout history and in the world today.

Our deepest beliefs tap into our survival instincts. When we hold a belief relating to freedom and justice, it's easy to react impulsively against a person whose belief differs from our own, because they represent a threat to our survival. Our emotional buttons are immediately and intensely activated and we automatically react. The more intensely held our belief is, the more emotional we feel and the more likely it is that the survival instinct is triggered.

The Formation of Beliefs

These are the primary ways our beliefs form and strengthen:

- They are handed down from our families, friends, teachers, leaders, politicians, news stations, loved ones, social media, or communities
- They develop through our experiences and our interpretations of those experiences
- They develop and strengthen through repetition of verbal and nonverbal messages
- They develop and strengthen through repetition and exposure to the same belief
- The quickest way they form is when they're combined with emotionally charged experiences

Accidental Hypnosis

Unfortunately, we're not taught how beliefs form. When we're unaware that we're being influenced, we're at the mercy of our own interpretations or misinterpretations, unscrupulous people, uninformed people, self-serving leaders, advertisers, and unintentional influences, including our own mind.

We don't realize that we're at risk of developing inaccurate and potentially harmful beliefs. We don't realize that we might be misinterpreting the words and actions of others. We cannot know whether what is said or done by others was said or done intentionally or not. We may never know.

All of this is the breeding ground for what I'm calling Accidental Hypnosis. Once you understand what I mean by this phrase, you will understand how it happens. Then you'll never be blind to the power of Accidental Hypnosis in your life ever again.

To fully understand Accidental Hypnosis and recognize its presence in our everyday lives, we must understand three things:

- The nature of suggestion
- The effect of data, stress, and overload
- The state of hypnosis

ACCIDENTAL HYPNOSIS

We've seen examples of how certain experiences lead to overload, resulting in a suggestible/hypnotic state. We've seen how self-talk (self-suggestion) in those suggestible moments can become self-hypnosis and how beliefs are strengthened through imagination and repetition. We've seen how suggestion and hypnosis impact our decisions and beliefs about ourselves and the world in regard to relationships, food, and self-esteem. But it doesn't stop there. The more you understand, the more aware you'll be, and you'll notice it everywhere.

Now that you are clear about interpretations, beliefs, and suggestions, let's take a look at how the mind is affected by data, stress, and overload.

3

HYPNOSIS

*It's all about mindset. Nothing is negative.
Nothing is positive. It all just is.*
—Jenae Noonan

Jenae Noonan, left, MMA (mixed martial arts) National Champion, bronze medalist, model, and motivational speaker, reminisced about her first fight and her rise to success. She said that when her opponent punched her in the face, "It hurt! And my emotions took over." When she complained to her coach, he said, "She's supposed to punch you."

Jenae saw very quickly how powerful emotions are. She realized that she would have to redirect her emotions to fuel her goals, rather than allow her emotions to control her. That decision to stay focused on her goal, and the constant reminder to herself about why her goals matter, are what won her the title.

You may think of this as determination, but it's more than that. Jenae took the power of her emotions and used them productively. You know that heightened emotions make us more suggestible and put us in an emotional state; suggestions from ourselves and others have extreme power.

Can you see the similarities between Jenae and Dog and Evander? They all used the power of suggestion to fuel their beliefs, and they amplified it by using emotion. They may not have recognized they were accessing the light hypnotic state along with the power of suggestion, but now that you understand it, you can see it in action. They are living proof of how it's done, which means you and I can apply the same strategies in our own lives.

Hypnosis, Trance, and Suggestion

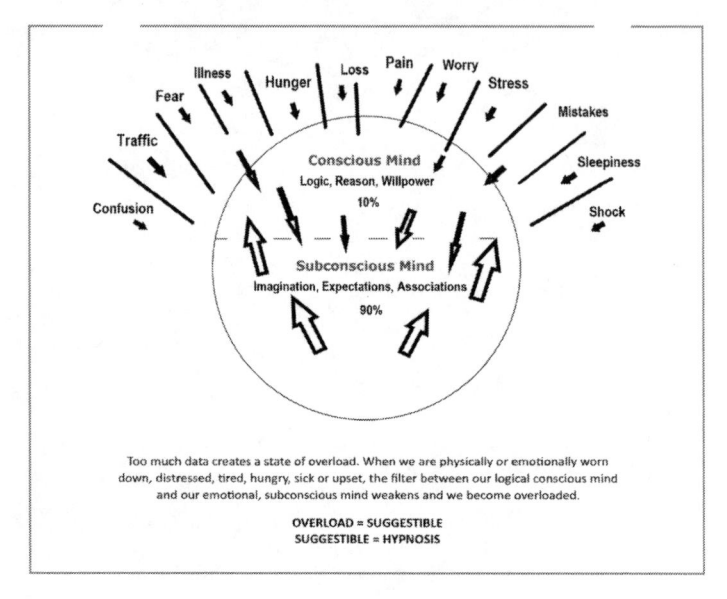

Diagram of the relationship between the mind, overload, hypnosis, and suggestion

Before we take a look at other forms of Accidental Hypnosis, let's look more closely at the brain, the mind, and how hypnosis is defined.

The brain cycles through different brainwave frequencies throughout the day and night. When we're working, concentrating, and actively processing information, we're in the beta brainwave state. It's the most active state. When we're winding down or sleepy, we move into the alpha brainwave frequency. It's a more relaxed state, where the analyzing ability of the mind decreases. We shift from alpha into theta, and then into sleep.

- We're least suggestible in the more active frequency of the beta brainwave state
- We're more suggestible in the alpha and theta brainwave states
- As we relax, the supervisor of the mind is less actively guarding what we're seeing or hearing, making the subconscious mind more available
- As we move between the alpha and theta brainwave states, we transition into a daydreamy state
- The daydreamy state is a hypnotic state
- When we're relaxing or when we're overloaded, we move from the conscious state into a light hypnotic, subconscious state
- Those are very familiar states to us because we travel between them throughout the day, and then into the evening until we drift off to sleep
- That drowsy state before bedtime is the **hypnagogic** state
- And when we awaken in the morning, we move from the sleep state to the awake state, which is the **hypnopompic** state

During the day, when we scroll through social media or daydream about a vacation or relive a worrisome incident, we also move back and forth from a beta state to an alpha state. Understanding this natural flow between the conscious and subconscious brainwaves is an important piece of the puzzle, and we'll refer back to this concept later.

The American Society of Clinical Hypnosis, the Society of Psychological Hypnosis, Division 30 of the American Psychological Association, defines **hypnosis** as: A state of consciousness involving focused attention and reduced peripheral awareness characterized by an enhanced capacity for response to suggestion.

Prior to the COVID-19 pandemic, when you heard a person cough, it may have barely registered in your mind. During the pandemic, you were probably keenly aware of every cough and sneeze you heard, and every unmasked person. If that person were standing behind you in a checkout line sneezing or coughing, your body would tense and your mind would become vigilant. More than likely, your imagination would be activated. Depending on how vivid your imagination is, your current degree of overload, and the frequency of their cough, your mind could easily slip into worst-case scenario thinking, or the "what if" loop. Those thoughts might trigger a panic attack or an increased level of anxiety.

Can you see how the imagination could become immersed in that experience, giving that cough or sneeze enough focused attention that it would immediately take you further into fear?

> As we relax, the supervisor of the mind is less actively guarding what we are seeing or hearing, making the subconscious mind more available.

The brain and body are connected. Thoughts and images connect to feelings. This is especially true when survival issues are at stake. Real or imagined threats set off the internal survival alarm.

Among the media's daily reminders of the illness and death count related to COVID-19, the stress of being unemployed or overworked, isolation from others, political unrest, and fear of the unknown, *it could be very common for the mind to want to escape or slip into imagination, and it happens in an instant.* The mind might remember hearing about people who were healthy one day and on a respirator the next day.

Spontaneous Accidental Self-Hypnosis

Can you see the strong similarity between this scenario and the definition of hypnosis: "A state of consciousness involving focused attention and reduced peripheral awareness characterized by an enhanced capacity for response to suggestion." The cough or sneeze is an indirect, unintentional (accidental) suggestion. It triggers the emotions and the imagination runs with it, which intensifies the feelings. The mind and body are connected, and every thought has a chemical reaction. That's why your blood pressure might rise just recalling a heated argument with a boss or someone you love.

Mayo Clinic describes hypnosis as follows: Hypnosis, also referred to as hypnotherapy or hypnotic suggestion, evokes a trance-like state in which you have heightened focus and concentration. Hypnosis is usually conducted with the help of a therapist using verbal repetition and mental images. In this state a person is more open to suggestions.[3]

All the definitions and explanations of hypnosis share a few elements: repetition and focused attention/concentration/repetition/trance-like state and an enhanced capacity for response to suggestion.

I remember a client who came to see me for help with depression. What the years taught me is that depression takes different forms. For some people, it's the result of brain chemistry. For others, it's a response to specific events or losses. And for many others, it's tied to a sense of hopelessness that results from the habit of repetitive, depressive thoughts. In this type of depression, a person gets stuck in a loop of repeated reminders of an upsetting belief, event, situation, person, or loss, which is replayed in their mind.

ACCIDENTAL HYPNOSIS

As the client and I sat together, I noticed that he was talking and smiling easily until he reminded himself that "Good things never last." Then he slipped down into the dark hole of depression. It happened right before my eyes, in a split second.

What I realized was that the problem wasn't that bad things happened. The real problem was that he kept repeating the bad experience in his mind, along with other bad experiences and the matching upsetting feelings. That made him even more upset, more overloaded, and more hopeless. I watched him as his eyes looked downward and his head hung, and he slipped further into that upsetting emotional state, reliving the chain of negative experiences. I could see that faraway look in his eyes as he recounted the stories, one by one, and simultaneously stepped back into the feelings. He relived the friendships that ended, the girls who broke up with him, and other losses that were not his choice. He believed his interpretation that once they knew the REAL him, they left. All of this became evidence that he was unlovable. He slipped into this depressive trance state right before my eyes in just a few moments.

Spontaneously and unknowingly, he slipped into the hypnotic state, accidentally using negative self-hypnosis and strengthening the feelings of depression.

You remember that emotion coupled with suggestion (when a person is overloaded) creates a hyper-suggestible state. That was exactly what was happening. And it was happening every day, many times a day. He did not even want to get out of bed because he felt so bad. And in his bed, he would review the upsets until they automatically populated in his mind. Naturally, the depression became so strong that he felt suicidal.

What was really happening was that he was spontaneously slipping into the hypnotic state and using Accidental Self-Hypnosis to strengthen his beliefs and the associated hopeless feelings.

The state of depression was automatic to his mind because it was repeated so often that it became an automatic loop, a conditioned response. He had no idea he was creating a conditioned response. The state of depression was familiar, and therefore it was a known.

You already know that interpretations and misinterpretations create beliefs. And in this situation, the depressive feelings grew out of the meaning he gave to negative life events, such as breakups, which his mind accepted as fact and truth. And that led to the beliefs that "There is something wrong with me"; "When people get to know me, no one wants to be my friend"; "No one wants me as their boyfriend because I am screwed up"; and "I am unlovable." And these beliefs continued to be strengthened by every story and hurtful emotion he replayed in his mind.

ACCIDENTAL HYPNOSIS

He was unintentionally cementing his depressive feelings and negative beliefs.

Can you see the connection between Accidental Self-Hypnosis and his feelings of depression? Can you see how the definition applies? He was strengthening his beliefs himself, unintentionally, because he was in Accidental Hypnosis every time he reviewed these kinds of situations in his mind.

I could talk to him on the conscious, logical level all day and night, but it wouldn't do a bit of good because he had built a protective wall around his perceived evidence that good things never last. It became irrefutable. And he was accidentally entering a trance state each time he recalled the upset, which transformed the self-hypnosis suggestions into an even stronger belief. This is a crucial piece of information and worth reading again and keeping in mind, because it happens to everyone, and it happens in the blink of an eye.

He couldn't see it. None of the psychologists or psychiatrists or therapists who had worked with him over the previous three years had seen it either. In fact, he went from therapist to therapist and, as each reviewed his history, he was essentially stepping into every upset and reliving the feelings over again and simultaneously restating his negative interpretation, inadvertently strengthening the negative self-hypnosis cycle. No one was able to pull him out of that state because they didn't understand hypnosis, so they didn't recognize what was happening.

This was a case of Spontaneous Accidental Hypnosis. He was spontaneously dropping into a suggestible hypnotic state and strengthening the upset and all the associations and negative beliefs, and then solidifying them in this state through repetition. The depression deepened and the beliefs became entrenched.

If the problem lives in the subconscious mind and it's being reinforced through the subconscious mind, then discussing it on the conscious level cannot change the feelings. It just helps the mind understand what happened, and why. But feelings and past experiences are tied to the subconscious mind, so they must be addressed in the subconscious mind. And that's exactly what needed to happen.

Spontaneous Accidental Hypnosis and Illness

Just as the depressed client spontaneously slipped in and out of a suggestible state, people diagnosed with cancer and those who love them, depend on them, or care for them also slip in and out of this state. One of the most vulnerable times we face is when we are diagnosed and being treated for a serious illness. Below is a quote from an article describing what happens when a person is diagnosed with cancer:

Fear of death, pain, or the recurrence of the illness of tumor patients can narrow their attention to a point where a spontaneous altered state of consciousness occurs.[4]

In another article written by the same author, he points out the relationship between stress and hypnosis and also how the medical world can make good use of the state of hypnosis.

During stress and hypnosis brain functioning is altered in a similar way, which can be seen both in the patient's symptoms and his/her physiological and neuroimaging findings.

... Hypnosis is characterized not only by physical and mental changes, but important unique social interactions as well. These interactions affect the endocrine and immune system and the mental state of the patient, they strengthen and synchronize resources and help posttraumatic growth. Since in the stress induced spontaneous altered state of consciousness the susceptibility to suggestions is increased, suggestive communication can be used effectively and it can even result in formal hypnosis induction. Under the strong time and mental pressure characterizing the work of the oncologic departments, it might help the staff to improve the cooperation with the patient if staff members, physicians, and

> *nurses are aware of the nature and the neurophysiologic background of the spontaneous trance state induced by the life-threatening diagnosis of cancer.*[5]

As a referral source for a highly esteemed cancer center, and I've personally witnessed this. The fear of death, the fear of side effects of treatment, the fear of the unknown, and the fear of recurrence are very real and are always lurking in the back of the mind. From the moment a person is diagnosed with cancer, the fear response and the imagination immediately go to work, pulling up the worst-case scenarios, and the "what if" dialogue begins. This is an example of Accidental Self-Hypnosis.

When we vividly imagine worst-case scenarios or listen to the stories of others while in a highly suggestible state, as we are when we're facing the unknown, we have increased responsiveness to suggestions. It doesn't matter if the suggestions come from us or from anyone else. The diagram below is a reminder of how overload creates Accidental Hypnosis and shows how the repetition of suggestions works to strengthen beliefs.

What your doctor says to you, the stories friends share, and what you imagine or tell yourself when you or a loved one is sick, can become very powerful suggestions. The more severe the illness and the more frightened you feel, the more powerful the suggestion becomes. Emotions tend to override the logical mind.

ACCIDENTAL HYPNOSIS

DATA COMING IN AND OVERLOADING THE MIND CREATES THE OVERLOADED STATE OF HYPNOSIS

CONSCIOUS MIND

CONSCIOUS MIND 1-12%
LOGIC
ANALYZING
WILLPOWER

SUBCONSCIOUS MIND

SUBCONSCIOUS MIND 90+%
IMAGINATION
EXPECTATION
ASSOCIATION

These lines represent suggestions

Each time suggestions are repeated they grow stronger

Over time they become beliefs that direct our behavior

Repeated Suggestions

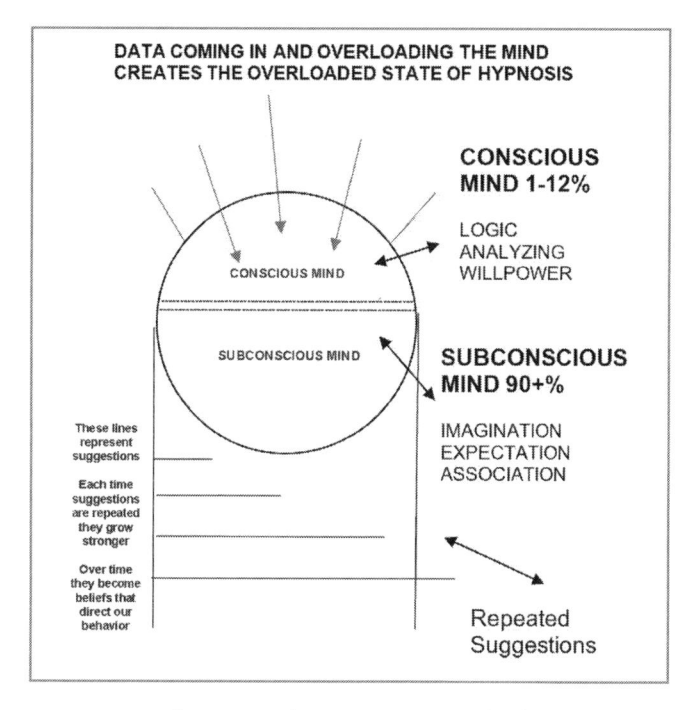

Strong emotions can create overload and lead to a suggestible state.

As you look at the photo below, notice the faraway stare on this young man's face. That "zoned out" look is essentially a trance state. In a way, he's left the room. You might notice the same look when strangers are in an elevator. Everyone is staring ahead, escaping the feeling of discomfort. That stare, that daydreamy state, that faraway gaze is such a normal, daily experience for all of us, which is why no one seems to think anything of it.

At the doctor's office, in the emergency room, or in a crisis situation, we tend to dissociate if we cannot manage the stress of the moment. Dissociation acts as an escape hatch when we have too much going on. But it's also a resting place for the mind. In itself, that's fine. But if we don't understand that we're in the hypnotic, suggestible trance state, we might find ourselves focusing on worst-case scenarios or replaying the past or revisiting depressing stories we've heard about other people with similar symptoms—all of which work against us.

The state of hypnosis is not the problem. How it's used can create problems. If we don't understand that we're in a vulnerable state and we don't understand the power of suggestion, then we are an easy target for whatever comes our way. And that's the problem.

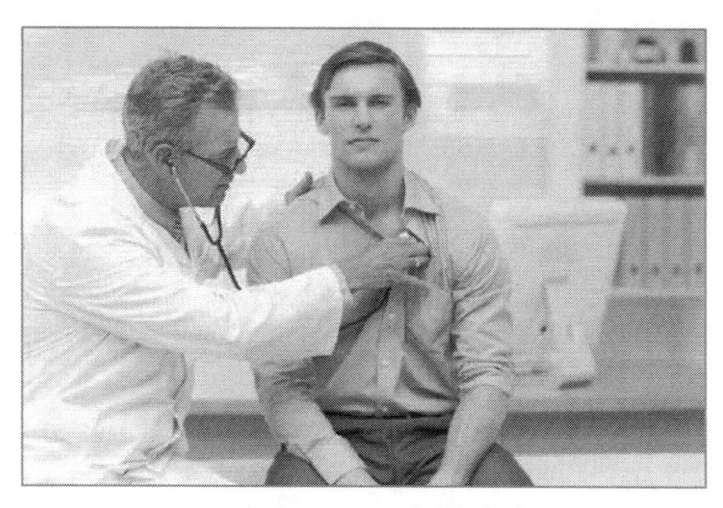

Notice the faraway stare on the patient's face.[6]

ACCIDENTAL HYPNOSIS

Mary was a client with a history of cancer. After her recent mammogram, the physician's office left an automated voice message asking her to schedule a mammogram. They also sent an automated email asking her to schedule another mammogram due to "incomplete findings." The call and email came at 5 p.m. Friday, so Mary had to wait until Monday to reach the office.

When a person has a history of cancer, there's always a fear of it returning. Seeing the words, "incomplete findings," and the request for another mammogram frightened her. Her mind immediately interpreted the information as *the cancer is back!*

She was sure it was cancer and supported her belief with what she considered to be clear evidence:

1. "Incomplete findings means something's suspicious, or they wouldn't ask me to take another test."
2. "It's obviously urgent because they emailed and called."
3. "They reached out at the end of the day Friday while I was at work because they didn't want to tell me the bad news and ruin my weekend."

How do you think Mary spent the weekend? Envisioning a slow, horrible death and leaving her children motherless.

The subconscious mind houses our imagination, expectations, and our past. That combination is much more powerful than the logical mind when emotions are high. That's why *what-If* and *worst-case* scenarios prevail.

When we're calm, we're able to look at the big picture and consider a variety of explanations. But when the stakes are high, logic takes a back seat to emotion.

The office staff called her first thing Monday morning to apologize and explained that there was a glitch in the system. They told her that her actual report of findings indicated no concerns at all. By the time Monday rolled around, Mary was exhausted. She had cried all weekend and was left with a headache from all of the tension.

The stress response is not just an emotional response. When we're under chronic stress it leads to physiological reactions, and none of them are good. Left unaddressed, chronic stress leads to a weakened immune system and a wide assortment of health problems. And so much of it is due to heightened suggestibility.

Medical doctors are highly respected authorities. Most people consider everything their doctor says to be factual. The information a doctor shares with a patient carries a high degree of influence. Over the years, physicians have become more aware of the power of their words, but many physicians, clinicians, and others remain unaware of such impact.

When we're in a holding pattern, waiting for information, or in transition, we're facing the unknown. Unknowns are very stressful because they are unfamiliar. Naturally we become overloaded. You already know that overload makes us suggestible to direct and indirect suggestions, our own thoughts, our imagination, and suggestions from others. And you know that when we add emotion into the mix, we become even more suggestible.

You also know that when we're sick or stressed, our ability to analyze well decreases and the more upset we feel, the more quickly suggestions bypass our critical thinking and drop into our subconscious mind. This is especially true for the negative suggestions because the brain is trained to make sure we survive by acting on important information. Now that you understand these concepts, you are better equipped to catch yourself and sidestep a treacherous path.

Summary

- When we vividly engage our imagination, we secrete the same chemicals as we would if we were actually experiencing what we are imagining. That's because it appears real to the mind, and there is a direct connection between the mind and body.
- When we couple a suggestion with strong positive or negative emotion, the intensity and impact of the suggestion multiplies.

- Ongoing worry and ongoing positive expectation are a combination of stepping into a future event and strengthening the emotions. Both have a profound impact but in opposite directions.

You now understand the link between overload and suggestibility, which is another way of describing the trance state (the state of hypnosis). And you know how it is that interpretations—accurate or not—are responsible for our subsequent beliefs. And that our repetitive thoughts and feelings directly contribute to our health and well-being. Can you see how this can create the breeding ground for a multitude of problems?

Next Step: Sometimes it's hard to tell if the problems that plague us are the result of Accidental Hypnosis. It might help you to ask yourself if you are dealing with any ongoing problems that seem unresolvable. These are problems that, no matter how hard you try to solve them, don't resolve. They just keep following you.

If so, Accidental Hypnosis might be behind it. For example, if you have a seemingly unresolvable problem, see if you can identify the underlying belief. It's easier to begin by dividing issues into categories such as relationships, career, family, and friendships and see if there are any repetitive patterns.

Let's use *relationships* as an example. If relationships are a problem, you might ask yourself, *What are my relationship goals?* and *Which relationship goals seem unattainable?*

Maybe your goal is marriage, but your relationships are short-lived. Maybe you keep attracting dishonest people. See if there is a pattern of feelings or experiences that are present in most or all of your relationships. Ask yourself if you have certain consistent feelings, such as jealousy. Then go back to the first time you had the problem and note any significant experiences that occurred before the problem began. Write down your top three beliefs around the problem. If you are having difficulty doing this yourself, there's a form on my website that helps you break it down.

Begin Here: Go to www.LauraTemin.com to download the **Belief Identification Form**. For the best results, finish reading this book before doing this assignment because you will have greater insight: https://www.lauratemin.com/forms-beliefs

For those who are struggling with weight or relationships, feel free to contact us to discuss whether our **Free Me Weight Loss System** or our **Spectacular Relationship Program** is the solution you've been searching for.

4

SABOTAGED

How do you know unless you look?
—Daniel Amen, M.D.

LAURA TEMIN

> ❝ Hypnosis is a powerful tool to enhance neuroplasticity and heal the brain and mind. As a master hypnotherapist for Amen Clinics, Laura Temin can show you how to use hypnosis to improve your brain and overall mental health.
>
> **Daniel Amen, M.D.**
> Dr. Amen is a world-renowned psychiatrist and a twelve-time *New York Times* bestselling author and the founder of Amen Clinics.

*If there's one person who thoroughly understands the relationship between the brain, the conscious and subconscious mind, nutrition, spirituality, and behavior, it's Daniel Amen, M.D., Founder of **Amen Clinics**, Inc. (shown above with me). Dr. Amen is a psychiatrist, neuroscientist, and twelve-time* New York Times *bestselling author. And he also knows the value of hypnotherapy to help calm and soothe the mind and build new habits.*

While this chapter is about the subconscious mind, it's also very important to understand the influence of brain function on behavior. Dr. Amen uses brain imaging to see what's really going on in the different areas of the brain. He's often heard saying, "How do you know unless you look?" and "Psychiatry is the only branch of medicine that doesn't look at the organ it treats."

Why is that important? There are two main reasons. First, because some symptoms masquerade as mental health disorders, but they're really medical problems. And if they're misdiagnosed, they never get properly handled. Our emotions and our behavior are also impacted by tumors, toxins, hormones, head trauma, and brain injuries. Psychiatric medications don't solve those problems. And not looking beneath the symptoms would be a tragedy.

And second, because seeing a scan of your own brain makes it obvious when brain-function issues are responsible for what looks like personality problems. Think about the difference that would make, if you thought your spouse was purposely being controlling and you learned it was due to overactivity in a specific area of the brain.

As you read this chapter, think about how brain-function issues might contribute to a person's problems. And think about how repetitive statements like, "You're lazy" or "stupid" or "selfish" might contribute to a person's beliefs.

Why the Cookies Win

Keisha was an account manager for a busy advertising firm. The demands of ongoing deadlines were part of her daily grind. She explained that her biggest struggle with weight loss was that, no matter how motivated she was and no matter how hard she tried, she would suddenly find herself off track. She would be on track and doing well, and the next thing she knew, she was eating food she shouldn't eat. The slip-ups always caught her by surprise. She didn't understand how they happened. This made her feel hopeless.

When she was working under the pressure of a deadline, there was no time to stop and eat, as every second mattered. She forced herself to put off eating until she had completed her work. Those were the two most important pieces of information that she shared with me, the telltale signs that revealed what was really causing the problem.

Keisha had a strong work ethic. She put her work above her personal needs. By the time Keisha completed her assignment and could finally eat, she was so hungry that it would be almost impossible to be discerning about what to eat. It's at that point that people reach for anything, especially those foods that they don't intend to eat.

There are scientific explanations for what actually happens in the brain/body system when we're hungry or tired, and the consequences of ignoring those signs. And while that information is essential, without understanding the relationship between the conscious and subconscious mind, we're missing a pivotal piece of the puzzle. That's why I address this and other key components in my Free Me Weight Loss System. Like most people, Keisha had plenty of information on diets. However, she didn't understand the relationship between certain foods and the reward system, as well as a host of factors that set a person up to fail, so she blamed herself for being weak.

The hours of work, the unaddressed hunger, the exhaustion, the stress, the pressure of meeting a deadline all together form an endless flow of data, relentlessly flooding the mind.

The more we have to deal with, and the longer we are dealing with it, the less analyzing ability we have in the moment. This puts us in an overloaded, hyper-suggestible state. Therefore, we don't have the bandwidth to be discerning. That makes us an easy target for anything in our path.

When the supervisor of our mind is on a break, no one's supervising our thoughts, feelings, imagination, or behavior. That makes us more impulsive. All the data that we're ordinarily able to filter out or put aside when we're not overloaded is no longer being well filtered because the filtering system is weak. *It's the filter that's* **weak,** *not the person.* That's an important distinction.

When we're *suggestible,* we're more easily influenced. It doesn't matter whether the influence is intentional or unintentional. It doesn't matter if the influence is positive or negative. It doesn't matter if the influence comes from inside our own head or from another person. The influence can even come from seeing or smelling a plate of cookies or an advertisement for cookies. When we're overloaded with more data than we can process, we are more easily influenced. Period. Exclamation point!

Our eyes may be wide open. We may be walking and talking and doing our work. But we're overloaded, so we aren't filtering as well as we would be if the supervisor of the mind were active. It's hard to concentrate when we are hungry. Our blood sugar levels drop and our analyzing ability is even more sluggish.

Just seeing a tempting treat can be a suggestion to eat one.

ACCIDENTAL HYPNOSIS

That's what Keisha was experiencing at work. And that's the state she was in on her way out the door, when she stopped by the break room to grab some water and noticed a bright-red box of cookies that were still warm. The smell was inviting. And sitting beside them was a handwritten note from her favorite co-worker, who loved to bake. The note read, "Please enjoy these homemade cookies while you can. They'll go fast!"

What do you think happened? Suggestions to eat those cookies bombarded her! She's *smelling* the cookies. She's *imagining* how good the cookies will taste. She's *seeing* the cookies. She's *remembering* the last time she enjoyed cookies that her co-worker baked. Her *body* is reminding her that she is hungry. And a sense of *urgency* is pressuring her to eat the cookies immediately because they won't last. And what happens next? Her *mind* convinces her that she's worked hard and deserves the cookies as a reward. These suggestions are coming from her own mind, her own body, and from her environment.

Notice how many indirect suggestions drew her toward the cookies. They certainly outnumbered that one single suggestion she gave herself: to remain on her diet. This kind of experience is what typically threw Keisha off her plan.

This is an example of Accidental Hypnosis, one that's a common experience among dieters. And it's completely misunderstood. Not only by the person on a diet but by friends, family, the fitness industry, coaches, nutritionists, and healthcare providers. Few of us realize the odds are stacked against us 90 to 10 when we're overloaded, and it's the overload that wears us down and makes temptation so much harder to resist.

When we're overloaded, it sets us up to fail. If we don't understand it, we *misinterpret* our behavior. We believe the lies in our head that tell us *we are weak*, when in fact it's our analyzing ability, our filtering process, and our energy levels that are weak in that moment.

Everyone's suggestible when they're overloaded. And everyone is suggestible to different degrees at different times and under different conditions. It's a normal human experience.

The control center of your mind is connected to the subconscious mind. Again, few people really understand how it works and how to make it work on their behalf. The key to solving that problem and related problems comes first through understanding *what's* happening, *why* it's happening, and *how* to intentionally use the subconscious mind and conscious mind to shift it.

Keisha believed she was making the choice to eat the cookie. She blamed herself and saw herself as weak because she could not say no, even when she wanted to say no. She said, "I am not strong enough." The truth is that our subconscious mind drives the choices we make as well as the physiological and metabolic components.

Our memories remind us of how delicious the cookies taste. Our imagination and expectations revel in the anticipated delight of eating those cookies. As a result, we feel compelled to reach for them in the moment, like Keisha. That's what happens beneath the level of awareness.

If we're able to win that battle and not eat those cookies in that moment, it doesn't mean we are safe and the door is sealed closed. We may have delayed reactions. We may successfully say NO to the cookies in the moment, but a day or two later they might pop into the mind once again. Or maybe during our next visit to the market as we pass the bakery, we grab some cookies there. Suggestions can be acted upon immediately, or they may accumulate in the mind before we respond to them. Delayed reactions are an example of the **Law of Delayed Action.**

> When you eat that cookie, you blame yourself for being weak because you don't understand it's not that you are weak, you're overloaded!

All these laws can be used intentionally for your benefit, but in many ways, they are also being used intentionally by marketing companies in every industry, and this practice is creeping in behind the scenes in social media, politics, and schools. It can be found almost anywhere. That's why it's so important for you to understand this concept.

When we're overloaded, we may not realize that we're suggestible because our conscious mind is still active. We don't realize that we're being driven by the memory or expectation or imagination. We can walk into the break room, like Keisha did, and have a logical conversation in our mind about not eating those cookies, and all the while the subconscious mind is working beneath the level of conscious awareness.

It boils down to this:
Hypnosis occurs when we are overloaded. Unfiltered suggestions are able to bypass our best intentions when we are in that suggestible state.

Most people don't realize that we give and receive suggestions all through the day, every day, throughout our lives. Here is what you need to remember about suggestions:

- They can be direct or indirect
- They can be intentional or unintentional
- They can be helpful or harmful
- They can come from our self-talk, from others, or from the environment
- They can be spoken, or implied through tone, facial expression, or gesture.

Suggestibility

We are particularly suggestible under the following conditions:

- When we have too much going on and it feels like more than our resources can handle at the moment
- When we're sick, in pain, tired, sleepy, emotional, or hungry
- When we feel threatened by real or imagined events (the mind treats them the same)
- During traumatic experiences
- When we recall traumatic or highly distressing incidents
- When we're drinking alcohol or using mind-altering substances

When we're suggestible, our ability to analyze is compromised. What's said or implied (even if it comes from us) bypasses our critical thinking. Such suggestions/interpretations drop unfiltered into the *subconscious mind* and ultimately influence our thoughts, feelings, behavior, and beliefs.

When we are overloaded, one of several things can happen.

- The imagination can run wild in a negative way
- The imagination can be used in an optimal way, using the overloaded state beneficially

- The mind enters the daydreamy, zoned-out state (hypnosis) to dissociate from the pressure

Faith is a beautiful example of how we can use the imagination in an optimal way. My mentor battled lupus her entire life. Every time she had a severe flare-up she was admitted to the hospital. Because she understood the power of suggestion and how the mind worked, she recognized when she was overloaded and used that suggestible state to imagine positive outcomes instead of outcomes that she feared.

She told herself that her heavenly father was watching over her, that she was safe, and that she'd heal quickly. Some people might say that's wishful thinking. But you know that we're always talking to ourselves, and that means we're continuously giving ourselves suggestions. Wouldn't you prefer to feel hopeful rather than have fearful thoughts chipping away at your physical and emotional health? When we're suggestible, messages that remind us that we've overcome difficulties before give us strength and hope that we can do it again.

I remember a visit home to see my family. I was working full-time, so I had to squeeze in a quick weekend visit. I rushed to the airport after a full day at work, so it was 9 p.m. before I was walking into my childhood home. I didn't realize this then, but when we go home, a part of us steps back in time. Not only do the memories and feelings flood the mind, but in some ways we regress into the parent-child relationship of our childhood. That's probably why you might hear a parent proudly say, "You may be an adult, but you will always be my baby."

My mother greeted me with a big hug. She asked if I had eaten and if I was hungry. She joyfully took me into the kitchen to show me the assorted foods she'd bought for me to enjoy during my visit. Many were foods I grew up on, like cream cheese and lox. And of course, there were potato chips and dips and salted nuts. On Saturday evening, she asked me, "Why are you so thirsty? Do you have diabetes?" My logical mind knew I was thirsty because most of what I was eating was salty, processed food. She said, "Diabetes runs in the family. Being thirsty is a sign of diabetes. When was the last time you saw the doctor? I think you need to have that checked when you get home."

I was dumbfounded that she could feed me salty foods and then ask why I was thirsty. Yet, multiple times she reminded me that I was overly thirsty and that it was a telltale sign of diabetes. Even though I knew the thirst was due to the salty food, her words raised questions in my mind. Why? Because I was overloaded after a long work week. I was tired after trying to squeeze five days of activities into two days. Therefore, her words bypassed my logical mind as doubt and fear slipped in. I began to wonder, *Am I excessively thirsty? Is it possible that I have diabetes?* I went from knowing I was fine to questioning my health. That's how quickly it happens.

False Memories

False memories are created in a similar way, by planting seeds of doubt or fabricating memories. You might be surprised at how powerful a suggestion can be when we're in an overloaded state. A 1997 study conducted at John Jay College of Criminal Justice found that if an innocent person were told that they were seen breaking a computer, they were more likely to admit guilt, despite their innocence, simply on the basis of another person's stating that they had witnessed it.[7]

Healthline describes false memories in this way:

> *A false memory is a recollection that seems real in your mind but is fabricated in part or in whole. An example of a false memory is believing you started the washing machine before you left for work, only to come home and find you didn't.*
>
> *Another example of a false memory is believing you were grounded for the first time for not washing dishes when you were 12, but then your mom tells you it was because you were disrespectful to her—and it wasn't the first time.*
>
> *Most false memories aren't malicious or even intentionally hurtful. They're shifts or reconstructions of memory that don't align with the true events.*[8]

> I remembered putting my phone in my bag. But I hadn't. That memory belonged to a different day and time.

The article goes on to explain the relationship between false memories and suggestion, as well as the powerful role *inference* has on our imagination. False memories can even be created by asking a question in a leading manner. Consider the concept of "leading the witness." Juries are influenced by the power of suggestion. Think about how this applies in your life.

Here's a personal example of a false memory. I was new to Georgia, and my best friend had come to visit. We left the house in a hurry and drove downtown to see a show. Parking was difficult, and it took forever to find a spot. When the show ended, I couldn't find my phone. I knew I had put it in my bag, but it wasn't there. We rushed back to the car to see if it was there. But it wasn't. We ran back to our seats to see if it had accidentally fallen out in the theater. It wasn't there. When my friend had the nerve to ask, "Are you sure you brought it?" I looked at him with daggers in my eyes and replied, "Of course! I clearly remember putting it in my bag like I always do." After retracing every step, we drove home. And there, on the dining room table, was my phone.

I believed that I had taken my phone. If I were to have taken a lie detector test, I would certainly have passed. I remembered putting it in my bag. But that memory belonged to another time. And that's why I try to remind myself that just because I believe something doesn't necessarily mean it's true.

5

REPETITION AND ASSOCIATION

As a physician, I know what people need to hear. The media knows how to capture eyes and ears.

—Dr. Drew

> Dr. Drew, here with me at CNN Center, spoke about what he learned early in his career as a physician trying to help people. He said that physicians who have a message to share need to know that "The priorities of people who create media are very different than our priorities. And that has to be OK with us because they know how to capture eyes and ears." Today, more than ever, this is an important message for all of us to keep in mind.

> Why? Because marketing is everywhere. The goal of marketing is to put a message in front of as many people as possible, over and over again, and strengthen it through emotions. Drama sells. Drama moves us.

> Those of us who aren't aware of what happens behind the scenes in television, radio, and marketing are easy targets. But awareness gives us the choice to turn off the TV, change the channel, or smile knowingly and hit delete. That power belongs to you. This chapter will reveal some of the hidden strategies regularly used to influence your life.

Learning, Advertising, and Laws of Hypnosis

Let's play a game! I'll write a sentence and you fill in the blank. Ready?

"*Like a good neighbor, ____ ___ is there.*" (Did you hum or sing that in your mind as you read it?)

What about *this?* "*For the best night's sleep in the whole wide world ____ _____*"

That's the **Law of Repetition and Association** in action!

One of the most popular advertising jingles is the famous Coca-Cola song "I'd Like to Teach the World to Sing," which dates back to the 1970s. That's an example of how powerful repetition and association are in cementing a message and brand recognition.

The Law of Repetition and the Law of Association are two of the most frequently used and most powerful laws of hypnosis, and they're also consistently applied in animal training, education, and marketing because they're *extremely effective strategies.*

Just turn on the tube and you'll see the same ads playing over and over again. Not just multiple times the same day, but for weeks and months and sometimes years. According to www.guinnessworldrecords.com, the longest-running commercial was aired in 1975, and as late as 2022 it was still running in some parts of the United States. The commercial says, "Thank You, Discount Tire Company."

Do you remember your ABCs? Did the singsong version of the alphabet song pop into your head? Do you realize that you spent years practicing your reading and writing skills? As children, we're taught to build associations by linking letters to words. A is for Apple, B is for Boy. We practiced every day. Repetition and association are two principles of learning, and they also happen to be the two most frequently used laws of hypnosis.

Advertisers know the value of repetition and association. And although repetition and association have been part of the educational system forever, for some unknown reason students are not taught to recognize this valuable concept or apply it in the world. How much better off would we be if we were taught in high school and college how these laws are used to lure us into smoking and drinking?

Think about beer and wine advertisements. They're filled with pictures of happy, sexy people drinking beer or wine. What do you think would happen to the sales if you saw that same beer or wine bottle broken on the bathroom floor beside a disheveled person with matted hair and vomit on their dirt-stained clothing? That would be unappealing. No doubt, beer and wine sales would plummet.

Over the years, I've seen how innocent rituals and repetitive behaviors led to lifelong battles with alcohol for so

ACCIDENTAL HYPNOSIS

many young people and adults. In my role as an independent Alcohol and Drug Evaluator and Treatment Provider for the Department of Behavioral Health and Developmental Disabilities, I've seen how peer pressure and suggestibility negatively influence a person's decisions. And over the last 20 years, in my private practice and as the only licensed therapist at the Amen Clinic in Atlanta, I've seen the profound effect emotional events can have on people. They create a state of overload, and trauma lingers long after an event ends.

Dr. Amen's single-photon emission computed tomography (SPECT) scans are able to detect the effect of highly emotional events. SPECT scans measure blood flow in different areas of the brain, and his research shows the ripple effect of trauma on a person's brain. It shows a behind-the-scenes correlation between brain function and behavior, which helps individuals and families reduce shame and blame as well as overcome denial.

Extreme emotional distress and traumatic events create a heightened state of suggestibility, particularly in the moment of the triggering event. With this in mind, can you see how the Laws of Repetition and Association could be an integral part of creating or prolonging problems?

> The symptom was not the problem. The real problem was hidden beneath the symptom.

Here's an example. Cici was in her 30s when she called my office for an appointment, stating that she was having trouble keeping up at her job and wanted help to gain more motivation and reduce her tendency toward procrastination. When she came in to see me, she explained that she was a single mom and she had a lot on her plate at work and at home.

What I found out was that Cici's lack of motivation was the result of poor sleep. She had trouble sleeping because a series of events from her early college years haunted her. And she drank every night to drown out the past and sleep.

The events were sexual acts she'd initiated as part of a sorority pledge. Particularly when we're young, our need for love, acceptance, and belonging is strong. Cici's desire to be part of the sorority allowed her to compromise her morals.

The experience was so traumatic that the memories continually haunted her. She couldn't help but relive the scenarios in her mind in vivid detail.

She was so ashamed of herself that she never returned to church. Can you see how much of a hold traumatic experiences have?

When people compromise their values and morals or make decisions they cannot face, it's not uncommon for them to disengage and stuff the upset inside. But stuffing doesn't solve the problem or make the upset go away.

It helps to remember that no one's perfect. Everyone makes mistakes and everyone has regrets. And when we let them linger or try to push them away, they just come out sideways or fester, eating away at our physical and emotional health.

If I had focused our hypnotherapy visits only on increasing motivation and decreasing procrastination, it wouldn't have helped, and neither she nor I would have known why. Too often, people describe their symptoms as if they're the real problem. Like Cici, they don't realize that lack of motivation, procrastination, drinking, and sleep issues may be tied to an underlying problem which has grown arms and legs. That's why it's essential that clinicians understand the differences. These and other overlooked concepts are an integral part of the curriculum at the Professional Hypnosis Institute. Our individualized approach with attention to the root cause creates excellent results for our clients and positions our students for success.

One reason hypnotherapy is such an effective tool is because it makes intentional use of the Laws of Association, Repetition, and Dominance, through therapeutic suggestion. When a person wants to break a bad habit (for example, nicotine), they muster up as much willpower and motivation as possible to make that change. That's the hard way to break habits or form new ones. When a person uses hypnosis to break a bad habit, we discuss their habit and rituals and their goal. We get clear about who they are as an individual and how they learn. We formulate goal-oriented therapeutic suggestions and engage their imagination. We're using the relaxed, creative mind in hypnosis rather than willpower, which allows the person to comfortably breathe life into their goals. Through repetition, they develop new associations, changing the way they think, feel, and behave. The beauty of hypnosis and hypnotherapy is that it bypasses the resistance of habit and allows them to move into alignment with their goal.

When a person is overloaded (by COVID, fear, anxiety, etc.), the most important thing I can do is block their suggestibility because overload makes us hyper-suggestible. Blocking a person's suggestibility makes a huge difference in their everyday life. As we saw with Keisha, when we are overloaded and suggestible, it's harder to recognize or resist suggestions. That's why it's difficult to resist temptations. And that's why it's so important to understand the Laws of Repetition, Association, and Dominance, and to use them for a person's benefit.

CONDITIONING

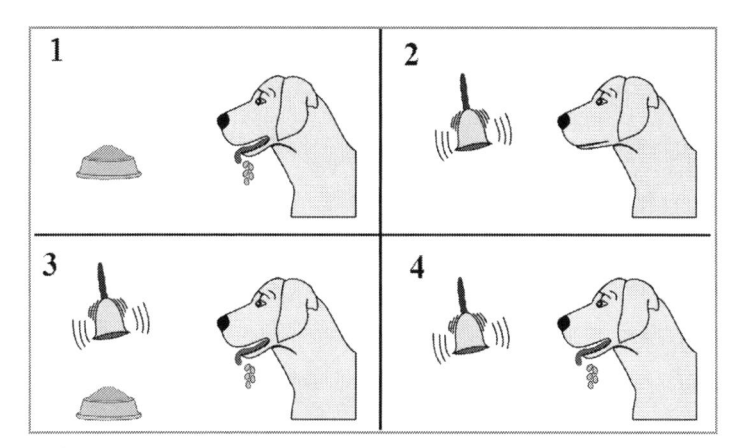

Conditioning is an essential element used in habit formation and habit change.[9]

The concept of Classical Conditioning was discovered by Ivan Pavlov in the 1800s. He found that by pairing unrelated stimuli became linked. He noticed that the dogs salivated when they heard the bell alerting them that his assistant had walked through the door with their food. The sound of the bell became associated with food. Over time, just the sound of the bell was enough to trigger their salivary glands in anticipation of being fed, without any food present at all.

This is the same concept advertisers use. Advertisers intentionally build associations.

- They pair their product or service with a specific need, want, or desire.
- They position their product or service as the solution to a specific problem.

Why is this important to you? Because as a human, you have wants and needs and heartfelt desires. That makes you a target for advertisers, politicians, scammers, and your own self-talk. If you don't understand how the mind works and you don't recognize the associations being elicited, you're more likely to be unfairly influenced, without your awareness or your consent, and potentially at your expense.

Today, advertisers have direct access to you through your personal inbox and your expensive smart phone. The news, advertisements, and social media feeds track your interests, habits, and preferences. They use and abuse that data to sell you products and services or feed or filter information that they decide you should have. Outside sources pay handsomely to place their messages in your mind. This is quite a problem, especially if you are clueless about the filtering process and you're in a light hypnotic state as you're scrolling. Remember that mindless scrolling puts you into a light hypnotic state, making you susceptible to unfiltered messages.

EXERCISE

Here's a fascinating exercise you can do every time an ad crosses your path. Pay attention to how the products and services are presented as *the solution* to any problem you might have. The Laws of Association, Repetition, and Dominance are everywhere.

The Law of Dominance says that we attend to the most dominant part of a suggestion. Think about the ads for medications; they use the Law of Dominance beautifully.

- The dominant message is the lion's share of the message.
- Because advertisers, including pharmaceutical companies, are legally bound, they offer a quickly stated disclaimer mentioning the negative effects of the medication at the end.
- The speed and volume of the disclaimer is completely different from the rest of the ad.
- The visuals are carefully chosen to emphasize the pain of people suffering with the disease that their medication treats.
- The final visual shows the joy of happy patients, their spouses, children, and pets, as a result of using the advertised medication.

Hypnotherapy

Over time, any neutral stimulus can create the same response as the original stimulus. This is what happened with Pavlov's dogs, and this is what happens for us in many aspects of our lives.

For example, people suffering from insomnia begin feeling anxious at bedtime. Bedtime becomes the conditioned stimulus. When a person has trouble falling asleep, just the thought of getting in bed or going to sleep becomes associated with the anxiety and fear of a poor night's sleep and a horrible day to follow. This further increases the feeling of anxiety. Now a person not only has insomnia but also the association and expectation of not sleeping, which creates a fear of not being able to sleep.

Because sleep deprivation makes it harder to think clearly, a person becomes even more suggestible. When they're worrying and imagining how bad they'll feel if they don't sleep, they are increasing the feeling of fear with each fretful thought. What they're accidentally doing is tapping into their imagination with "what if" scenarios that play over and over in their head whenever they think about sleep.

Fear and worry create a suggestible state, and that reinforces the thoughts and feelings of fear and worry. People become caught in a cycle of Accidental Self-Hypnosis and unintentionally strengthen what they don't want. That's part of what keeps them stuck in the insomnia cycle, but they don't know it.

Many people have no idea that hypnotherapy is such an effective, drug-free option for insomnia. They're desperate for sleep, so they ask their physician for sleep medications, and because sleep is so valuable, they don't care or don't remember that the medication is only meant for short-term use. Not many physicians understand how the state of hypnosis and hypnotherapy can be used to help their patients.

William Dowdell, M.D., and Hitendra Patel, M.D., have each held the position of medical director of the Sleep Disorders Center at the Wellstar Hospital System. Not only do these knowledgeable and caring physicians provide full medical workups, using sleep studies to diagnose health concerns such as sleep apnea or restless leg syndrome that affect sleep, but they also consider the possibility that stress, anxiety, or other emotional concerns might be a contributing factor. Should they find that the sleep disorder has emotional components, they confidently present a referral list to the patient which includes hypnotherapy options along with psychology and psychiatry. Many people choose hypnotherapy over traditional counseling when their doctor makes the referral and understands the benefits.

> If a suggestion creates a problem, then suggestions delivered in the right way can resolve the problem.

It was a blessing for me to have worked at the Wellstar Hospital System and to have had the opportunity to sit in as a welcome participant at the monthly sleep-disorder meetings. The meetings included physicians specializing in neurology, dentistry, and pulmonology, along with respiratory therapists, and mental health clinicians. They brainstormed difficult cases and shared their knowledge and perspective. Those monthly meetings taught me so much about sleep hygiene, sleep apnea, restless legs syndrome, night terrors, narcolepsy, and the medical perspective of sleep.

I'm forever grateful to these doctors for their openness to hypnosis and hypnotherapy. It was Dr. Dowdell who put in writing a request that the gift shop carry my hypnotherapy audio recordings to help people sleep. While many hospital systems remain tied to old traditions, I have found that the Wellstar Hospital System embraced a collaborative approach to health care. Because of the physicians and administrators who understood the value of whole person care, we were able to include hypnotherapy in the programs for the inpatient psychiatric hospital and in their outpatient clinic.

The Bottom Line: If a connection is created by the subconscious mind, then it must be resolved in the subconscious mind. If a suggestion created a problem, then the right suggestions, delivered in the right way, can resolve the problem. As a licensed psychotherapist, marriage counselor, Integrative Clinical Hypnotherapist and Founder of the Professional Hypnosis Institute, it's my experience that hypnotherapy is the fastest and most soothing way to extinguish old beliefs and dissolve or replace old conditioned behaviors. It's especially useful for problems that have been unresponsive to standard methods.

6

HIDDEN HYPNOSIS: ADVERTISING AND ALCOHOL

Addictions neither respect nor spare anyone. College is usually a person's first experience with freedom. Youth need to be educated to be prepared.

—Candy Finnigan

Candy Finnigan (right), A&E TV interventionist, speaker, and a voice of hope and wisdom, took me down memory lane. She explained that she and her husband had developed a lifestyle of drinking. Drinking was wearing her down, but she had no intention of stopping, until her mother-in-law threatened to take her children from her unless she stopped. That forced her to make a decision that changed her life.

Most people have their first experience with alcohol during their teen years. No one starts out as a heavy drinker. It all begins with a sip. People find that alcohol helps them relax, deal with stress, feel less awkward, quiet the chatter in their mind, feel part of the crowd, or escape something they don't know how to manage. We all want to feel better, so it's easy to see how a habit can form. After a while, alcohol and other substances have the ability to create physical and psychological dependence, and addiction takes over.

Can you see how a habit can become an addiction through the Laws of Repetition and Association? We associate the drink or drug with having fun and feeling better. And we repeat the behavior. As you read this chapter, you'll see how we're targeted from youth and throughout our lives.

Hypnosis is a natural state. When a person is in the state of hypnosis and we offer a therapeutic suggestion, it is a welcome gift. Remember a time when you had an argument with someone and that person said very hurtful things to you? Remember how bad that felt? Now remember that you told a friend what happened, and your friend reassured you that what was said wasn't true. They named all of your wonderful qualities and reminded you of the many good things you've done. Of course, you felt better. That's the therapeutic use of suggestion. You didn't know you were in a suggestible state, but you understand that when you are upset or tired, you're suggestible.

Advertisers use suggestion all the time. Think about Nike. Their tag line is "Just Do It." Their ads tell stories of a person's dream becoming a reality. They show everyday people and superstars wearing their shoes and achieving their dreams. They use suggestion to encourage you to take action and remind you that you have power (in their shoes).

The state of hypnosis is not the problem. It's how that state is used that can create a problem. That's why it's important to understand how advertisers use suggestion to influence you.

Advertising — An Insidious Form of Accidental Hypnosis

We don't typically look at advertisements when we're fully engaged and focused at work or when we're actively involved in a task. We're more likely to look at advertising when we are winding down for the day or scrolling on the internet in the evening after the day is done, or when our mind is tired and we need a break from work, and of course while watching the tube. There are three things to know about advertisements and suggestibility.

#1. All advertisements are direct or indirect suggestions. You already know that suggestions are most powerful when they touch our emotions. Advertisers know they must tap into our emotions, our needs, our desires, or our fears in order to move us to action. They target our basic human needs and wants. Think about what most people want. The list usually includes the desire to be loved, accepted, healthy, happy, safe, attractive, fulfilled, accomplished, and financially secure.

#2. Sales tactics involve moving us toward pleasure and away from pain.
The advertised product or service will either solve a problem or fulfill a desire.
The primary strategy advertisers use is to identify a problem or desire and offer their product as the best or only solution. The goal is to build a positive connection in your mind between what they have and what you need so that

you make a purchase. Most advertisers don't directly state that you will be loved, have great sex, become popular, be confident, or marry the person of your dreams if you purchase their product, but they sure do imply it. They use the power of suggestion in nonverbal forms, particularly through images.

#3. "A picture is worth a thousand words" is an old adage for a reason.
Research tells us that communication is a combination of verbal and nonverbal elements. The nonverbal aspect is the lion's share of communication, especially when verbal communication has word-count limitations, such as on Instagram and in advertisements. We have become such a fast-paced people, with a shorter and shorter attention span, so the optimal way to get a message across quickly is through images.

ALCOHOL

An easy place to begin is with alcohol advertisements, because they typically connect their product to sex, popularity, fun, relaxation, and confidence. All advertisements target specific populations and design their advertising for their target audience. Men have been a target market for the beer industry. Over time, women have gained advertisers' attention for both beer and wine. The type of advertising designed for men is distinctly different from the type of advertising created for women. Similarly, advertising that targets youth is different from that created for the more mature adult market.

An employee of a major marketing firm shared a little secret with me years ago. She said it's common practice to test commercials before running them. And she then revealed that their agency tested ads by placing electrodes on the heads of male research volunteers to see how aroused they become while watching certain beer commercials. Once the information is gathered, they run only those advertisements that produce the highest degree of arousal.

This is a very intentional ploy to excite the pleasure centers and connect that good feeling with their brand. Doesn't this appear to be a way to build an association of pleasure with a particular brand? Although the advertisers don't call it hypnotic suggestion or intentional hypnosis, they are applying the same principles in a very sneaky way. Doing so ensures that an unsuspecting viewer has a "pleasing" association with their specific product or service, thereby increasing the odds that they will purchase the product.

> Using the power of suggestion and the Laws of Hypnosis, advertisers' market to men, women and youth by linking their products with sex, love, acceptance, and popularity.

If you think it's only done with alcohol, think again. These tactics are widespread, but we are unsuspecting victims, directed and controlled without conscious awareness. That's the problem. And what's worse is that we think/believe/assume that *we* are the ones making the decision to ask for that beer or a "full bodied" wine or a "smooth" scotch by brand name when, in truth, we've been played and cleverly programmed by sneaky, sophisticated marketing professionals.

By intentionally tapping into the emotions and desires when people least expect it and dropping in a suggestion, the advertiser is willfully influencing the thoughts, feelings, and behaviors of a person who is relaxed and drifting off into a fantasy, completely unaware of what's taking place.

That's the power of suggestion. It isn't the respectful form of hypnotherapy that helps a person reach a goal, solve a problem, or break a habit. It's the kind of hypnotic suggestion that you need to be alerted to, so when you see it coming, alarms will sound and you can **avoid** the influence.

Can you imagine how many people are blindsided and taken advantage of by *accidentally* entering the state of hypnosis and being conditioned by repetitive messages? Research shows that anxiety has increased since COVID-19's emergence and that there's been an increase in alcohol consumption and weight gain. Based on what you've learned so far, you know this is not a coincidence.

ACCIDENTAL HYPNOSIS

When we're afraid, isolated, and depressed, most of us eat and drink more to soothe ourselves. Drinking breaks down our analyzing filter, so it's harder to have just one drink. Eating carbs and sweets soothes the anxiety centers of the brain, but the overload of sugar leads to inflammation, illness, and addiction. And when something is designed to taste good and tap into the pleasure center, the mind and body crave more. It's no secret that food manufacturers hire scientists to make foods as appealing to our taste buds as possible. In too many foods, they intentionally use little to no fiber. Fiber is what helps us feel full, and without it we are going to consume more. Looking behind the scenes is essential if you want to be fit and healthy.

Since so many suggestions are visual, let's take a peek at some examples of subtle and obvious suggestions tying alcohol to relaxation, fun, and sex. I've included this exercise to help you build awareness so you can see the concept in action. The goal is to foil the attempts of tricky advertising and make the decisions that are best for you.

Instructions: Look at each photo below. Take note of your first impression. Does it remind you of a good time with friends or loved ones? Do you have a negative or positive association with it? Based on the goal of advertising (to solve a problem or fill a need), see if you can determine what the primary message is. In fact, you can work toward blocking your suggestibility if you commit the following three questions to memory and make a habit of answering them for every ad you see. Doing that will activate your analyzing ability and help stop you from being played.

Each time you see an advertisement, ask yourself these three questions and then give yourself the following suggestion:

- Question 1: What do they want you to buy? (e.g., My Brand Wine)
- Question 2: What images or statement are they stating or implying will promote pleasure or pain? (e.g., My Brand Wine has no sugar—message is that you won't gain weight. And the image is of a gorgeous, smiling, fit woman in a bikini with a handsome, fit man beside her on a yacht.)
- Question 3: What message do they want you to believe in order to sell their product? (e.g., You can be that woman, or have that woman, and a great life and never get fat and enjoy wine, so buy My Brand Wine.)
- Suggestion: Then make this statement to yourself, *"I'm much too smart to be fooled!"*

ACCIDENTAL HYPNOSIS

Alcohol Ad—Beer and Sunset[10]

This photo is a great example of how an advertisement can make use of subtle suggestions applying the Law of Association. If you glance at it quickly, you may not notice anything in particular. But let's analyze what's shown. There are two people, each with a bottle of beer in their hand, making a toast. They're outside, in nature. In the background is a lovely sunset. What feeling does it promote? What does this say to you?

The meaning you make is based on whether you have a positive or negative relationship with alcohol. An advertiser who wants to entice a consumer to buy their product may choose this photo because the sunset indicates the day is over. The intended, implied message might be, "It's the end of a busy day and it's time to relax." Nature is relaxing and soothing for most people, and this builds an association between a relaxing and soothing experience and their product. A toast can imply a celebration, a connection between friends, family, buddies, or lovers. The message is vague enough that you can give your own meaning to it, yet the overarching nonverbal message is for you to relax with a beer. Beer equals relaxation, beauty, time to celebrate, good times, special people.

Remember, normally when we look at ads, we're not analyzing them. We see them for a moment, usually during a leisure activity, and often at the end of the day, when the mind is less active. The mind is not intently focusing or analyzing when we are mindlessly watching the tube or social media or turning the pages of a magazine. We may simply notice the sunset, the drink, and the toast. It gets processed in the mind very quickly. The initial reaction might be "It looks so relaxing," which leads to "I want to feel like that!" which leads to "I want a beer!"

Thoughts run constantly and quickly through the mind, as we are busy doing other things, so we're often unaware of them. And we may not even reach for a beer in that moment. But if we meet a friend for dinner later that day or the next, we may think, *I would like a beer.* It may seem like the idea and the decision are our own, but are they? Perhaps the idea was suggested by an ad seen earlier that day or the day before or through ongoing suggestions we constantly receive.

If we don't have the immediate response of reaching for a beer, but we reach for a beer or a drink later that night or within a few days, we might see the Law of Delayed Action at work and the result of a post-hypnotic suggestion. If we order a different kind of alcoholic beverage, we may have generalized the suggestion to apply to all alcohol. To increase the sales of alcohol, the advertiser knows they must repeat the same ad or similar ads with their branding, making use of conditioning and many of the laws of hypnosis.

Brainwave States

The next crucial bit of information is the effect of brainwave states. So let's add that into the equation. You know that the mind cycles through active and inactive states throughout the day, between waking and sleeping. And you remember that the mind is in the beta state when we are actively engaged in thinking but moves toward the alpha state when we relax. Isn't this the time we are scrolling through advertisements or watching the tube? You know that when the mind is tired, it automatically looks for relief, so it naturally slips into a daydreamy state. Isn't that when we take a break from work? And isn't that also when we're scrolling or engaging in mindless activities? Remember that we move through the hypnopompic and hypnagogic states every morning and every night. When the day is done, we are moving toward that sleep state, and that is a suggestible state because we are sleepy or tired or winding down and the mind is naturally less analytical.

It's no surprise that we eat snack foods at night and we drink wine or beer at night or on a weekend when we're relaxing. Many of the commercials we see on TV are about food and drink, and we are watching it at the end of the day or when we want to relax. Also keep in mind that most of us have our smartphones at our bedside.

Many of us reach for our phones first thing in the morning and last thing at night. Isn't that when we are in a light hypnotic state? We're more easily influenced at this time. This is typically when we're browsing social media or catching up on emails and unaware of the influence of unintentional and intentional suggestions.

We'd all be better off if we decided to stay off-line until after we completed the one most important task of the day, whatever that might be for each of us. And we'd feel better and accomplish more if we used that light hypnotic state intentionally. Perhaps using self-hypnosis to stay centered or reinforce our goals. You can protect yourself from the impact of Accidental Hypnosis by keeping this awareness in mind.

ACCIDENTAL HYPNOSIS

Alcohol Ad: Good Head

This ad is much less subtle, and its intended market is different from the relaxation message shown previously. It's not a real brand or a real ad; I fabricated it by combining other real ads of the same flavor and enhancing them. It's probably the kind of ad that could pop the electrodes off the head of many men. Do you think it's a coincidence that the woman's face is missing? It's hard to miss her full bosom as she leans in. The positioning of the beer and the carefully chosen words just below her breasts add to the intended fantasy.

The goal of this advertisement is to build a positive association between the advertised product and sex. What if the ad showed a very old, unkempt woman with sagging breasts that hung to her navel? Do you think it would have a positive effect on the pleasure center of the brain? How many beers do you think it would sell?

LAURA TEMIN

Chasing a Memory of Fun — Addiction

Matt was shorter than most of the boys his age and was quite shy. He felt awkward around people he didn't know. The guys liked him, but his height was the brunt of their jokes. Parties were a nightmare for him until he discovered the magic of beer. After that, all his inhibitions disappeared and he became the life of the party and he felt part of the crowd. By the time he was 19, beer had become a staple in his life. He never imagined that he would pass out at the wheel while driving his friend home.

Alcohol use, abuse, and dependence is a big problem in the United States and throughout the world. As stated previously, just like the tobacco ads that target young people, so do many of the alcohol ads. They intentionally build a connection between fun and drinking or fun and smoking or vaping.

Fact: None of the people who seek out help with drinking or smoking ever intended to become addicted or to be controlled by alcohol or other substances. Often, people drink in an effort to solve an underlying problem, such as sleep, awkwardness, or to forget the past. In the beginning, teens experiment with drugs and alcohol because they're curious. They want to have fun, be part of the crowd, and feel more grown up. Isn't that the message the ads present? People drinking and smoking and having fun!

The *habit* of drinking develops over time, just as any habit does. When thoughts and actions become habituated, the mind pulls up the thought, "A cigarette/a drink sure would be good or help me now." When we have a good experience, the mind remembers that when we are in similar situations. Each time we act on it, our self-suggestion becomes a more automatic thought in the mind. And over time, the suggestion moves from *It would be nice* to *I want*, and eventually to *I need*.

With alcohol, the person remembers the good feeling and they're looking to repeat that experience. But when a person develops a problem with alcohol, they no longer have the experience of fun that they remembered. Instead, they're chasing the memory of fun long after the fun experience ended. Isn't that what happened with Pavlov's dogs? They salivated at the sound of the bell because it was associated with food, and their minds anticipated and responded physiologically to the memory and expectation of the food.

When something becomes a habit, it's because the thought and the behavior have become automatic through the reinforcement conditioning. The belief that alcohol is fun or relaxing or satisfying has long been established through repetition, and over time, it becomes integrated in the person's mind. When a person becomes physiologically dependent on alcohol, their body demands it. Dependence naturally occurs over time. It's not a reflection of a person's character. Alcohol dependence does not mean a person is a bad person. It's simply a physiological response to the continued use of alcohol.

> When the conscious mind and subconscious mind are at odds, people feel stuck, because they are!

The brain's filter doesn't fully develop until approximately age 25. That's one reason teens and young adults are such an easy target. Everyone wants to have fun, fit in, and relieve boredom and stress. When a person can't stop drinking, they blame themselves for a lack of willpower. But you and I know that the odds are stacked against them. You can read more about alcohol and addiction in my interview on the topic for the *Jewish Times*.[11] And you can also read about how alcohol affects the brain at the National Institute of Health website.[12]

> **TIP:** If you're an addictions counselor or would love to make it easier and more comfortable for a person to drink less or quit drinking completely, our hypnotherapy certification program includes Specialty Training on alcohol use, abuse, and addiction. You'll be surprised at the difference it can make in reducing cravings, anxiety, and stress, helping them stay on track

Therapists, addiction counselors, and those already in the helping fields will find that this training provides drug-free, healthy alternatives that work along with standard treatment to support people in freeing themselves from addiction. It is a comprehensive approach using hypnotherapy to gently address trauma, habit, brain function, and cravings. People desperately need qualified, caring, and nonjudgmental help.

Shauna was drinking more than she wanted to drink and, despite her desire to drink less, she just couldn't control herself. She told me she was working full-time. She had a very demanding job and a young child. She was the breadwinner. Although her husband was also employed, he was home much earlier and refused to participate in "women's work," which included keeping up the house and helping with their daughter.

She told me she was depressed and frustrated. She felt endless pressure at work, at home, and as a mom. It's natural to seek relief from pressure. Relief and escape were the gifts that alcohol provided. But drinking was causing other problems. She uncomfortably admitted she was drinking a bottle of wine every night and falling asleep on the sofa. She was embarrassed that her husband and daughter saw her in that condition, and she didn't like feeling foggy the next day at work. She was suffering, her weight was increasing, and her effectiveness at work was declining.

Can you see the bind Shauna was in? Her conscious mind knew that drinking was causing a problem but her subconscious mind was seeking relief. Which part of her was going to win? The 90 percent subconscious mind or the 10 percent conscious mind? When the conscious mind and subconscious mind are at odds, people feel stuck, because they are! Unless they are able to resolve the conflict, they remain stuck.

> Her conscious mind knew that drinking was causing a problem but her subconscious mind was seeking relief.

We used the conscious mind to discuss her goals and make a plan. We used hypnotherapy to calm and soothe Shauna's subconscious mind. Hypnotherapy helped weaken her desire to drink and strengthen her ability to communicate with her husband. We reinforced her goals and action steps in hypnosis. Once the conflict was dissolved, life became more manageable and the drive to drink diminished.

Too many people struggle with habits and addictions due to an internal conflict. We can talk about it on the conscious level, but that may not change the feelings. Our feelings and thoughts drive our behavior. Although people know they should drink less, knowing and doing live in different parts of the mind. Antidepressants and anti-anxiety medications may help us worry less, but they don't solve the underlying problem. Ultimately, we have to take a more comprehensive approach.

7

HIDDEN HYPNOSIS: FOOD AND THE AMERICAN DREAM

Give people the facts, but deliver your message in a way that gets people emotionally engaged.

—Dr. Mehmet Oz

> *Mehmet Oz, M.D., (seen on the monitor), live here with me, is a board-certified cardiothoracic surgeon and professor emeritus of surgery at New York-Presbyterian/Columbia University Medical Center. He is an author and medical device patent holder.*
>
> *Dr. Oz is passionate about helping people improve their health. Many health issues benefit from diet or lifestyle change. And change is difficult. Dr. Oz smiled as he paid tribute to Oprah Winfrey, quoting what she had told him early in his career: "People don't change based on information. They change based on how they feel."*
>
> *If a person has a heart problem or diabetes and needs to lose weight, but they diet and fail, and they diet again and fail again, they develop a negative association with dieting. Just thinking about dieting makes them feel bad because they remember all the times they tried and failed.*
>
> *Dr. Oz knows that when we ask people to do something they can do, they will do it and feel successful. And each time they take action and succeed, they become more confident and more motivated to continue taking action. Dr. Oz applies the power of emotion and positive conditioning to motivate people toward their*

goals. And, like Dr. Amen, he understands the value of hypnotherapy. The last time we met, Dr. Oz shared his views on hyp in the med arena, stating, "It's one of the most underused tools. And it's remarkable that something as demonstrably useful as hypnotherapy is ignored so frequently.

As you read this chapter, you'll learn how advertisers use emotions and the state of hypnosis to get us to buy their goods and services. Once you understand, you'll know how to sidestep the traps, and you can use the same tools for positive results.

Laura Temin LPC, LMFT and Dr. Oz / College of Physicians

Targeting Youth

Asia sat on the sofa in front of the television, mesmerized by the screen. Beside her was a box of her favorite cereal, Fruit Loops. Asia had already eaten a waffle with butter and maple syrup for breakfast, about an hour earlier, but she was hungry again. And as she watched her favorite show, she ate handfuls of brightly colored sugary cereal, right from the box, washing it down with a Kool-Aid Jammer. Dr. Amen, he understands the value of hypnotherapy. The last time we met, Dr. Oz shared his views on hyp in the med arena, stating, "It's one of the most underused tools. And it's remarkable that something as demonstrably useful as hypnotherapy is ignored so frequently."

A variation of this scenario happens every day. Not just with Asia but with children, teens, and adults in every city and every state across the nation. Sugar-filled breakfast foods and snacks are a health disaster that begins with undercover marketing. (Read about sugary drinks in this CNN Health article—see note.[13])

When kids are parked in front of a screen watching a show or a movie, they are in a trance state. You can see the faraway look as they stare at the screen. Kids spend much of their time in trance states because they can't filter well yet. That's why they are such an easy target for marketers. Parents don't realize that everything their kids watch potentially affects them and may shape how they see the world.

Antoine recalls that his family ate dinner together every night. During the fall of 1967, the TV evening news featured heavy coverage of the Vietnam War. Even as a 59-year-old man, Antoine remembers the horrific scenes he saw as a child at the dinner table, and how nauseated it made him feel. The vision of young men with their legs blown off fighting a war was so emotionally distressing that he couldn't eat. Those horrors and those nauseous feelings became associated with dinnertime, and over time, grew into his feeling nauseated and unable to eat at the dinner table, and then spread to any table at dinnertime. This is an example of the Law of Association and the power of Accidental Hypnosis.

> **When kids are parked in front of a screen watching a show or a movie, they are in a trance state.**

The associations we make can be positive and soothing or negative and distressing. For some people, chocolate chip cookies aren't just cookies—they are tied to the feeling of love and to grandma, who had fresh baked cookies at every visit. This is the power of Accidental Hypnosis.

Sugar Addiction[14]

Targeting begins with preschoolers and follows us throughout our lifetime. Marketing magic and omission strategies (which are explained later) contribute to addiction, obesity, inflammation, and a host of emotional and physical problems. And it's all done for the almighty dollar, without concern for the ill effects on the consumer.

Did you know the original name for Frosted Flakes cereal? In 1952, "Sugar Frosted Flakes," a breakfast cereal for children, was introduced in the United States. But in 1983, the word "sugar" was removed from the name, although the sugar content remained the same. Why do you think they removed "sugar" from the brand name? Probably because that's when it became public knowledge that consuming sugar causes serious health problems. And obesity, especially in children, was on the rise.

Eden David of the ABC Medical News Unit illustrates how the food industry targets youth and describes how advertising is intentionally used to influence choices. You may be surprised that they point out the connection to the unconscious mind and the reward system of the brain. I've highlighted some main points below, but you can read the article at the link for this note.[15]

Food Target—the Teen Market[16]

- The food industry spent about $14 billion on advertising in 2016. Adolescents are considered a major market and, therefore, they are targeted.[17]
- Fast food ads are designed to activate a teen's brain on a subconscious level.

- More than 20 percent of 12- to 19-year-olds are obese.
- Unless targeted marketing is addressed, the obesity crisis will continue.
- The greater the exposure a child has to food branding, the stronger their connection to the brands and the more likely they are to eat those foods.[18]
- There's global evidence that producers of unhealthy food, drinks, and alcohol are using the COVID-19 pandemic to market their products through COVID-washing.[19]

The Temptation Train

While all advertising is meant to lure us, food advertisers are notorious for using manipulation tactics, such as omission and confusion, to coerce us onto the temptation train. The best way to think about food advertisements is to think about a runaway train filled with all of your favorite foods and happy people joyously partaking, continuously inviting you to join them.

The goal of the advertiser is to entice you, your children, and your loved ones to hop on board and stay there for eternity. Every word, every facial expression, the music, the background, the images are designed for this purpose. The temptation train runs 24 hours a day, 7 days a week. It stops at your door multiple times a day.

As a person who spent decades addicted to sugar, I know firsthand how difficult it is to break free, particularly when we are intentionally and unknowingly baited. And once we are trapped in the sticky web of addiction, it's hard to break the cycle. Every day I work with people who are incapacitated by their weight. It affects every area of their lives, emotionally and physically. Severely overweight people tend to socialize less and isolate more. Over time, they just feel hopeless. But they don't know that they've been set up and played because they're unaware of the hidden deception strategies in place.

Benjamin was 6'2" and weighed over 250 pounds. He had diabetes. He had pain in his joints and, at age 45, he was walking with a cane. He knew what to eat and what not to eat, but he couldn't resist stopping at the fast food restaurant for a biscuit and a shake. He would drop his son off at school, pull up at the drive-through window, and place his order. He ate in the car because he was too ashamed to go inside.

It's much easier to head off a problem than it is to undo a problem. Many of the emotional and physical weight-related issues people struggle with are the result of advertising which was designed to slip under our radar. This puts us on that temptation train, which eventually becomes the addiction train, and finally the illness and depression train. Since we can't fix what we don't understand, let's identify and dissect the strategies advertisers use to pull us in and keep us trapped.

Partial Truth, Confusion, and Omission Strategy

The name *Partial Truth, Confusion, and Omission Strategy* really sums it up. This approach is frequently used in advertising of every kind. It's also a staple in politics. This strategy is a mainstay for the food and beverage industry. Each of these components can be combined or used separately. The purpose is to influence buying behavior.

Consider the following terms: natural, grass-fed, free-range, no added sugar, sugar-free, zero trans fat, fat-free, lite, gluten-free, naturally sweetened, lightly sweetened. They're intentionally misleading. They give the impression that a product is healthy when it's not. With this tactic, the manufacturer lures the unsuspecting consumer into believing that they're making a positive health-conscious choice. Read this article "16 Most Misleading Food Labels"[20] for an overview of food labels.

Below is an example of partial truths, confusion, and omission in this Hershey's Special Dark Kisses ad. Ask yourself, who is this ad targeting? It seems to me that they are targeting an adult population who may already have high blood pressure or be concerned about it.

Fight High Blood Pressure

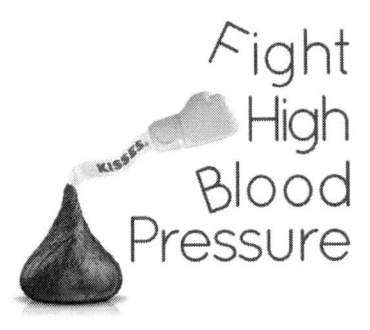

With Hershey's Special Dark Kisses you can improve blood flow and help knockout the formation of blood clots. Studies show that eating a small amount of dark chocolate two or three times each week can help lower your blood pressure.

Hersheys.com/Kisses

HERSHEY'S

Let's dissect this advertising strategy—the facts and the ingredients—so you can see behind the smoke and mirrors.

Strategy: The ad makes a claim that Hershey's candy fights high blood pressure, a serious health problem. But does it really? Notice that ad is using the Law of Association and the Law of Dominance. They use the Law of Association to connect their candy with health. The Law of Dominance says that we pay attention to the strongest part of a message. The large-sized print in the heading reads, "Fight High Blood Pressure." Here we have an ad that intentionally omits information in an attempt to convince us that because dark chocolate fights blood pressure, their candy is a healthy choice. That's omission and confusion in action. Can you see how they appear to address a health concern, but it's really a self-promotion strategy?

Fact: Hershey's ad implies that this candy is dark chocolate, but it is not true. That's why they can't call it dark chocolate. They have to call it Special Dark Kisses. And Special Dark Kisses have none of the benefits of the research behind the dark chocolate claim. Read the ingredients and the facts related to the ingredients below, and you will see how they purposely use confusion and omission to trick us into buying their product, thinking it promotes health.

Ingredients as written on Hershey's website's ingredient data:

1. Sweet Chocolate
"A chocolate prepared by mixing chocolate liquor with a sweetener, such as sugar. The U.S. Food and Drug Administration (U.S. FDA) requires sweet chocolate to contain between 15 and 35% chocolate liquor."

2. Sugar
"The term 'sugar' can be used to refer specifically to sucrose, or it can be used generally to refer to all simple sugars (lactose, glucose, fructose, galactose, sucrose, etc.)."

3. **Cocoa Butter**

   "The naturally occurring fat obtained from cacao (cocoa) beans either before or after roasting. Cocoa butter is a unique vegetable fat extracted from cacao (cocoa) beans or chocolate liquor. Its unique fatty acid composition, including palmitic, stearic, oleic and linolenic acids, provides the pleasant mouthfeel and flavor release of chocolate products."

4. **Milk Fat**

   "The fat that occurs naturally in milk. Also referred to as butter fat."

5. **Cocoa Processed with Alkali**

   "Cocoa powder that has been treated with alkalizing agents to reduce the bitter flavor, resulting in a milder tasting cocoa when compared to cocoa powder. Also known as Dutched Cocoa."

6. **Lecithin**

   "A substance found in the oil component of certain plants that acts as an emulsifier, to prevent ingredients from separating."

7. **Natural Flavor**

   "Flavor derived from a spice, fruit or fruit juice, vegetable or vegetable juice, edible yeast, herb, bark, bud, root, leaf or similar plant material, meat, seafood, poultry, eggs, dairy products, or fermentation products of these."

8. **Milk**
"A white, fluid beverage produced from dairy cattle. A source of nutrients, including protein, and calcium."

Fact: The Hershey's ad implies that their product fights high blood pressure, but according to Healthline,[22] the best dark chocolate has a 70-percent or higher cocoa percentage. Hershey's has only 36 percent, which is not disclosed on the package, and it's much less than what qualifies for the benefits of dark chocolate.

Fact: Hershey's Special Dark Kisses are made with cocoa that is processed with alkali. This is called the Dutching process, and it is known to have negative effects on the antioxidants in the dark chocolate and significantly reduce them.

Fact: Dark chocolate of the highest quality is made mostly with cocoa; therefore, cocoa would be listed as the main ingredient. But Hershey's Special Dark Kisses lists cocoa as the fifth ingredient. And it's processed with alkali, as stated above.

Remember, we all suffer from wishful thinking. We want to believe that it's perfectly fine to eat the foods that we enjoy, even when we know better.

Advertisements like the one above try to use research to fool us. They give us permission to eat something that can harm us and tell us it helps fight disease. If we believe their lies, we are able to use research to support our self-suggestion to eat chocolate.

If you're interested, you can read the facts about added sugars and what is healthy in the Healthline article at the links shown in this note.[23]

Read the AHA recommendations at the website link shown in this note.[24]

You can also review the actual ingredients in Hershey's Kisses at the link in this note.[25]

Addictive by Design

Manufacturers deliberately design foods to be addictive. "A Healthline survey showed that nearly half (45 percent) of people are surprised to learn that sugar has the same addictive characteristics as heroin, cocaine, meth, and nicotine."[26]

When we eat sugar, the brain releases dopamine, *a feel-good chemical*, which stimulates the desire for more sugar. Sugar also releases serotonin, which makes us feel happier. When something tastes good and makes us feel good, we naturally want more of it. Unfortunately, when we eat too much sugar, we have too much serotonin in our system and our system stops producing serotonin. As a result, we may wind up with a deficiency of serotonin, and that can lead to depression. Even sugar substitutes (both the healthy and unhealthy) tend to trigger our cravings for sweets.

Behind the scenes, eating the sugar makes us feel good and want more. The cocoa butter and other fatty acids in Hershey's Special Dark Kisses provide a so-called pleasant mouthfeel. The sugar gives us a boost of energy and then our energy drops, so we reach for another chocolate kiss to feel better. The brain remembers the good feeling and taste, activating the reward system, and we repeat the process over and over again.

Weight problems have many contributors. One that people don't often consider is the role of brain function on behavior. When we know we should not eat something but we can't stop ourselves it may be due to the intentional addictive design of the foods or brain function issues. These make it harder to stay on track with a diet or eating plan, even with the best intentions. Often, people with stressful jobs, busy lives, and not enough sleep are hit hardest. Because they're already worn out, they're easy prey for advertisers. Remember Keisha? Repeated suggestions, in the form of commercials, internal body cues such as hunger or anxiety, as well as visual stimuli (seeing other people eating food we like, or just seeing a sizzling juicy burger) act as triggers. Advertisers attempt to activate all of our senses, making it harder to refuse the foods we promised ourselves we'd avoid.

> Most diet programs, fitness professionals, and medical experts don't understand the subconscious mind or its influence on decision making.

We don't realize that the advertiser is dropping in waking suggestions that are intended to tempt us. We don't know that brain chemicals are driving our desire, so we blame ourselves. It seems like we're unsuccessful in our diet because we are weak, which gets that negative self-talk ball rolling down the slippery slope of hopelessness. And when we feel bad, we tend to reach for something that makes us feel better—something sweet or something else that creates a cascade of feel-good chemicals. And every time we get off-track with our diet, we perceive it as evidence that we will never accomplish the goal, which reinforces the belief.

Remember, when we're tired or stressed, the brain looks for energy or a boost. We're not analyzing *why* we are reaching for sweets or breads or pasta or the foods that turn to sugar, but late-night snacking is often the result of being tired. When we're tired, we look for energy. We don't realize that's what's driving us. We aren't consciously telling ourselves, *I'm tired. Let me eat something and get some energy.* We're simply fighting to stay awake because we want some "me time" at the end of the day or we want to finish the movie we're watching or complete some work that is due.

When we reach for those foods, not realizing what we are looking for, remember that we're looking for energy, or even that we saw the Hershey's ad and received its permission to eat the Kiss, that it sets us up with the belief that it's OK to eat it. And once we get off track, we tell ourselves, *"I already broke my diet, so I might as well just finish it off. It's too late now."* We might also tell ourselves that we're hopeless, and we'll never be able to reach our goals, so why bother. Remember, when we're tired or feeling emotional, we're more affected by suggestion, and the power of those suggestions is multiplied.

Unfortunately, most diet programs, fitness professionals, and medical experts don't understand the subconscious mind or its influence on decision making, so they can't share this information. They address weight from a purely logical perspective, with food restriction and exercise. But you know that logic diminishes when a person is overloaded, hungry, and suggestible. Those programs fail this group of people, and most chronic dieters fit into that category.

That's why I developed the Free Me Weight Loss System, with specialized tools for people whose diets have failed. This program is available to clients, and I offer the professional version to other clinicians. The Free Me System arms people with the tools and information needed to avoid

Accidental Self-Hypnosis, sidestep the weight-loss landmines, and feel emotionally empowered to succeed.

Counter Sales and Add-On Sales

Gas station checkout counter—lottery ticket is sitting on the left by the lighters to tempt us

Strategic Placement: Lottery tickets, cigarettes, vape pens, candy, and anything else that is strategically placed at a checkout counter are more indirect suggestions intended to influence you and encourage sales. Placing lottery tickets at the checkout counter as shown above is an *implied*

suggestion, reminding shoppers of the unlikely chance they can win millions, and be, as they say, "Set for life." Winning the lottery equals riches and the freedom to live as you choose, which triggers the desire to buy a ticket and take a chance (before you leave the store and miss an opportunity)

Consider the names of the games: Mega Millions, Fantasy 5, Lady Luck, Cold Hard Cash, Cash Eruption, Lucky Loot. The odds of winning are less than one in a million. But the focus is on the chance, the dream, and the imagined lifestyle, because as you know (through repetition), "You can't win it if you're not in it."

Those who are feeling grounded, those who aren't hungry or tired, may not be baited by the lure of the dream or the draw of snacks and junk food. And *because they are not overloaded, they might remember all the wasted money they've spent on lottery tickets and will smile and say no.* Remember, a suggestion is a suggestion, and each person gives meaning to suggestions.

We move toward pleasure and away from pain, and we're more impulsive and less likely to evaluate well when we're overloaded If you can remember this at the checkout counter, you can smile and say, "No thanks!"

Facts

- "Lottery retailers collect commissions on the tickets they sell and also cash in when they sell a winning ticket, usually in the form of an award or bonus."
- "Time and time again, when a lottery was introduced in a state, the local number of adults who engaged in gambling (which a lottery technically is) increased 40%."
- "An overwhelming amount of lottery participants seem to reside in the lower economic classes, according to the stats."
- "Consumer-finance gurus say the lottery is essentially an extra tax on the poor."

Can you see how the power of suggestion is at work with the lottery and counter sales? Read the article at the link shown in this note.[27]

8

HIDDEN HYPNOSIS: POLITICAL PERSUASION

Just because you do not take an interest in politics doesn't mean politics won't take an interest in you.
—Pericles

Television is a four-minute universe.
—Marc Siegel, M.D.

Marc Siegel, M.D., seen here with me, is a Professor of Medicine at the NYU Langone Medical Center, a Fox News Medical Correspondent, author, and internist. Dr. Siegel shares so many nuggets of sound advice around science, politics, medicine, and media, and all of them also apply to our lives in general

He said, "People are never who you think they are. And one of the biggest mistakes in our world right now is that people are interpreting all the time through video screens, through print media, through some snippet, and making determinations and thinking they know the person, and then they project that all around the world."

Wow. That is the gift of an insider's perspective, and it's worth remembering. You know from the chapter on beliefs that we often confuse feelings with facts. And we don't even realize it's happening. Today, more than ever, we must remind ourselves that what we see, hear, and read about people is skewed to some degree.

In a world of constantly changing information, it's hard to know what's valid and current and what isn't. We only believe that what we heard—that our source—is trustworthy and in the know, but we only know snippets of the truth. Dr. Siegel also reminds us, especially in regard to COVID-19, "The science is still evolving. This is a big problem when the world is trying to understand and treat a new disease."

He warns us that so much of the information we've been told previously no longer applies. But too often we, the public, are left swimming in fear because the media isn't diligently sharing corrections when new information arises.

Listening to Dr. Siegel, I realized that it takes time, dedication, and a high degree of personal integrity to review the research objectively. But isn't that true for so many things. One way to remove our personal bias is to take the time to investigate the facts quoted, from all sides, before we share or discount what we heard — even when it comes from a source we trust. If everyone did this, we'd all be better off.

Fear, Worry, Persuasion

This chapter is going to push a lot of your emotional buttons. As you read this chapter, pay attention to your stress level, your thoughts, the things you're saying to yourself about what I am sharing, and even how it might deflate or inflate your opinion of me. Pay attention to your body. Are you physically tense? Do you feel anxious? Whatever you're feeling and thinking is a small-scale version of what you've been dealing with, inside and outside, particularly over the last few years. We're so busy managing the ongoing and debilitating stress of our lives as the new normal that we often don't realize the impact the political climate has on our stress level, our physical and emotional wellbeing.

Politics is a touchy subject, and we're warned to stay away from it. I'm going to do my best to write about what makes us so sensitive and reactive, and try not to pit one side against another and alienate anyone. My purpose in discussing this is that it is the biggest emotional elephant in the room, so I have to address it. And my hope is that by understanding what actually creates and intensifies our emotions, we gain perspective, which allows for a greater sense of inner peace.

Everyone has their own beliefs and opinions. Each one of us believes that what we think and feel is right and that those who disagree with us are either uninformed, biased, or just plain stupid. What makes our opinions so strong is our personal life experiences, combined with our interpretations of what we see and hear. Remember, our experiences and our interpretation of those experiences are what build and feed our beliefs. Most hardwired, firmly held beliefs are the result of what's near and dear to our hearts.

The issues that connect or divide people exist around liberty, justice, equality, freedom, fairness, choice, health, safety, protection, money, taxes, power, control, weapons, the earth, the world, human lives, and immigration. It's our personal relationship with these issues that steeps us in our positions. And in so many ways, these are life-and-death issues, so of course they are going to push our buttons.

Consider this scenario. Person A says, "I support fairness and justice for all." Person B says, "I support fairness and justice for all." But what Person A sees as fair and just might be very different than what Person B sees as fair and just. They agree on the concept, but the disagreement is in how the principles are applied and enforced.

Person A's daughter is a single mom of a five-year-old boy. Person A's daughter works full-time in a busy accounting office. Her days are long, so Person A takes care of the child while her daughter is at work. Person A's daughter has a heavy workload and must meet monthly deadlines. One day, her boss insists that she work late to ensure that they meet their upcoming deadline. When she finally leaves the office, she stops at the market to pick up a sandwich. She calls her mom to tell her that she'll be home within the hour. Three hours later, she still isn't home. Her mom, Person A, is increasingly worried when her daughter doesn't answer her phone. At midnight, a police officer shows up at Person A's door, informing her that her daughter has been killed in a head-on collision with a drunk driver. Person A is devastated.

As a result, Person A now firmly believes in zero tolerance for people driving under the influence. She is adamant that anyone driving under the influence should be prosecuted to the full extent of the law.

Person B has been out of work for six months after her business closed due to COVID. She's also a single mom with a child. After three months of unemployment, she's gone through all the money in her savings account, which had taken years of hard work to build. Due to the pandemic and its effect worldwide, she is behind in her rent and her car payments. She's been driving for Lyft and working at Dollar Tree, taking day and night shifts just to make ends meet and pay for her child care. Her credit cards are maxed out because she's using them to pay the utility bills and keep the lights and electricity on in her apartment. She's paying high interest rates and her debt is mounting. Her only living relative is her retired aunt who, despite her moderate income, has been helping Person B pay her rent. Person B finally lands a government job with benefits. When her aunt hears the news, she invites Person B out to dinner to celebrate.

ACCIDENTAL HYPNOSIS

They enjoy an early dinner and each of them drinks one glass of wine to celebrate. As Person B pulls out of the restaurant parking lot and onto the street, her handbag, sitting at the edge of the passenger seat, begins to topple over. As she reaches to catch it, her car swerves somewhat, and a police officer who is driving by notices her swerve and pulls her over. When she rolls down her window, the officer smells the alcohol on her breath and asks if she has been drinking. Although she insists that she had only one drink and that she is not impaired, she is given a citation for driving under the influence (DUI). Her car keys are confiscated and her car towed, and she is taken to the police station.

As a result, her employer retracts the job offer. On top of that, the law requires that she get a clinical evaluation by a state-approved drug-and-alcohol evaluator to determine whether she has a substance-abuse problem. The evaluation costs her over $100.

> We see the world through our own eyes and ears and interpretations. But with issues of the heart, there is little room for compromise.

The clinical evaluator tells her, "Everyone who is charged with DUI must attend treatment." The evaluator then files her report with the probation officer along with a recommendation requiring Person B to attend a treatment program for a minimum of four to six months. Person B does not know that it isn't true that every person charged with DUI must attend treatment. She does not know that she is entitled to get another evaluation. And she does not have the money to hire a lawyer to fight on her behalf.

The entire experience has been not only unfair but also embarrassing and humiliating. She believes she was unfairly accused, taken advantage of, misjudged, and treated like a liar, an addict, and a hardened criminal. She has been saddled with additional financial burdens that she believes are due to a dishonest system and extremely unfair laws. It has taken more than a year for her case to move through the courts and another eight months before she has satisfied all the requirements. In the interim, she was forced to file for bankruptcy because her job options diminished due to the DUI charge on her record. Person B is adamant that the laws are not fair and are just another way for the government to get more money.

Can you feel the pain in both scenarios? Can you see why each person feels so strongly and believes their point of view is right? If you have friends or family on either side of that experience, you're probably having a stronger reaction than someone whose life has not been touched in this way at all. Fairness and justice are completely different to Person A and Person B. *And that's the way it goes for all positions, all topics, and all people.* We see the world through our own eyes and ears and interpretations. But with issues of the heart, there is little room for compromise, and that example illustrates why.

Politicians intentionally take advantage of emotional triggers to intensify our connection to their political stance, and to create negativity around their opponent and the opponent's position. Politician A and her media/network emotionally force-feed us only scenarios that fan the fire and support her stance and disparage our opinion of Politician B. And Politician B and his media/network emotionally force-feed us only scenarios that fan the fire and support his stance and disparage our opinion of Politician A.

Personalizing their positions with emotionally elevated stories draws us in much more than facts. Here's an example of how this works.

- Position A—Zero Tolerance:
X number of people die from automobile accidents every year. Help us keep our roads and families safe. Vote for Politician A.

- Position B—Responsible Drinking:
X number of people are needlessly charged with DUI every year because zero tolerance laws are too extreme. They tie up the courts and

waste taxpayer dollars. It's an unfair means of increasing revenue. Vote for Politician B.

Did the statement of fact move you more than the story about Person A and Person B?

Statements of facts and figures are important to support a person's decision to choose one candidate over another. To vote for or against one bill over another. But it's the story—the personalization—that brings the concept home. And the goal of the political party is to make us feel like they are on our side. That they understand and support our positions. And to promote a sense of confidence that this person and this political party will fight for our rights.

The most powerful way to move a person is to engage their emotions. The best movies and the best books introduce a gut-wrenching storyline where the main character (the good guy) tries to accomplish a goal but encounters difficulties and ruthless villains along the way. He overcomes these obstacles, fights the villains, and comes out the winner. All movies have storylines, but the best movies pull us in so that we become engrossed in the story and feel connected to the character as if they were a real person.

What we don't recognize and never expect is that politicians also follow the *storyline game plan*, and it goes like this:

"I, the good politician, am your hero. I represent YOU. I will fight for you and I won't let you down. My opponent is dangerous and evil and not trustworthy. He will destroy everything of value to you, to us, and to our world. Your participation in this election on every level is crucial to the future of your children and grandchildren and the world. Together we won't let the bad guys take advantage of you/us anymore. This is an urgent situation and it requires you to do the right thing and vote for me. I will protect everything that matters to you."

> The politician touches all possible pain points to rile us up and then swoops in with their solution, as if to save the day.

As we listen to our politician, the words they say and the topics they address, we are made to feel that they are sincere. Remember, we experience our feelings as facts, and the political-writing campaign strategist knows this. We are intentionally made to feel as if they know and care about what matters to us and they will be our voice. They stand a certain way. They use gestures in a certain way. They pause after certain words. They speak *seemingly* from the heart. But we don't realize that what this candidate is saying was designed by expert speech writers and that every move and every word is orchestrated. *It is designed to move us.*

The politician touches all possible pain points to get us riled up and then swoops in with their solution to save the day. They speak the words that soothe our concerns and promise that *they can and will deliver us from this horrible situation*. All they ask is that we vote for them and follow their advice in all matters. Then everything will be OK. But if we don't obey, beware—the villains will win and take over the world and no one will be safe. In fact, it's your responsibility to do as we say, because otherwise you are endangering everyone.

If you look at political positions throughout history, you will see variations of this ploy being used on both sides to different degrees. Because both political parties (the one you support and the opposing party) have done such a masterful job, you might believe that what I expressed above is not true. You might see it as true for the opposing side but not for your side. I promise you, if you look back in time and ahead in time and listen for this—on a topic that does not push your emotional buttons—you will hear it in every campaign, on every issue, on every side.

Every issue a candidate or politician discusses will follow some variation of this outline. Most government mandates and health guidelines also follow this formula. Sometimes it's for the good of the people. Sometimes it's for the good of the politician or for some unknown, behind-the-scenes individual, group, or purpose. It's hard to know until long after they're in office, and sometimes years or even decades later.

ACCIDENTAL HYPNOSIS

You already know that when we're overloaded by stress, worry, fear, and situations we can't control—when our freedom or our survival is threatened or when we experience trauma—the mind naturally escapes into hypnosis because hypnosis is the flight part of the fight or flight response. And you know that we're easily influenced when we're overloaded. You know that the greater the emotion, the more suggestible we become.

Between the COVID-19 pandemic and the 2020 presidential election, many people became paralyzed by fear. Real fear and *imagined fear*. And you remember that the brain releases a chemical reaction to our thoughts and feelings, which travels throughout the brain and body system in response to what's real as well as what's imagined. The stress response weakens our immune system and makes us more vulnerable to illness. Yet we're still being bombarded multiple times a day with fear and worry messages that pop up on our phones, in our emails, on TV, and in the news. Fear of the future, fear of death, fear of illness, fear of others, fear of laws, fear of leaders, fear of a new and experimental vaccine, fear of not getting the vaccine, fear of known and unknown side effects from the vaccine, fear of people not wearing masks, fear of people shedding, fear of decreased oxygen levels and declining memory from continual use of masks. Fear of the unvaccinated. Fear of the vaccinated.

We're fearful of other people whose opinions differ from ours. We are fearful of looting and riots, fearful of the police, and fearful of not having the protection from the police. We are worried about the value of the dollar and worried about not having enough money to pay our bills. Gas prices are rising. Supplies are decreasing. And people are concerned about access to essentials, including food, water, and toilet paper. Many parents are fearful that their children aren't getting the kind of education they need, or that their business won't survive.

So many of us are facing heavier work demands, longer hours, unemployment, and personal conflicts. Our values and our finances are pitted against each other when we have to decide between staying home with government subsidies or working and earning less. Throughout the quarantining parts of the pandemic, many parents had the increased responsibility of attending to their family while managing their workload and the difficulties of being in tight quarters, day and night, with everyone stuck at home. We've been eating and drinking more as we remain socially distanced and alienated from loved ones and communities in times of celebration and illness and need. And on every level, we are overloaded.

> Despite how far-fetched that idea sounded to me, it turns out that data manipulation is a known problem.

ACCIDENTAL HYPNOSIS

It's this state of environmental, waking hypnosis, that makes us extremely emotionally reactive. Even people who were known to be polite and patient are no longer monitoring what they say. The filters are dissolving. Facebook friends, real-life friends, and neighbors have grown extremely vocal and intolerant. Why? Because everyone is concerned about health, freedom, justice, and the future. Yet, behind the scenes, we're being triggered by political divides, racial divides, news and media divides. We're bombarded by injustices, censorship, intolerant influencers, loudmouths, and know-it-alls, and we are all becoming more judgmental. Look at how quickly and how deeply this divide has progressed. The media, our political parties, and our respected leaders continue fanning the flames of emotion to get us to stand with them and follow their lead.

Strategies of Persuasion

Our politicians and leaders apply the same tactics that the food and alcohol advertisers use: partial truths and omission strategies, the Laws of Repetition, the Laws of Association, and the Laws of Dominance. Just as the goal of the advertiser is to get you to buy their product without full transparency about the harm it can do, politicians also have an agenda.

Our elected representatives took an oath to be our protectors and work for us, not the other way around. Yet, when you stand back and look calmly, none of it appears to be in our best interest.

Over the years, I've been very fortunate to know and work closely with researchers, physicians, and clinicians. In graduate school I was required to take a class in statistics. I formerly believed that numbers were numbers and the numbers told facts. I believed the inserts that came with the medications were verified facts. I believed that if someone quoted a study, that information was inarguably factual. I believed all studies provided information that was based on facts. If my doctor shared information with me, I believed the doctor was quoting the facts. But one physician/researcher I met shared some information with me that opened the door to understanding statistics from a different perspective. He said that data can be and often is manipulated. Intentionally and unintentionally. *What?* That was completely incomprehensible to me. How could data be manipulated? Data are just facts, right? But is that true?

Despite how far-fetched that idea sounded to me, it turns out that data manipulation is a known problem. How and why does it happen? On the website Social Care Influence for Excellence we're told, "The misrepresentation of research findings may arise for a number of reasons. It may be willful, dishonest, accidental, partisan, political, ignorant, biased, careless or any combination of these." The article continues, "Common ways in which research findings are misrepresented are explored under the following sub-headings: flawed research, using findings out of context, stretching findings, distorting findings, rejecting or ignoring findings." Read more using the links shown in this note.[28]

Under the heading "Misuse of Statistics," Wikipedia advises that if we ignore important information, we come to faulty conclusions:

> *Multivariable datasets have two or more features/dimensions. If too few of these features are chosen for analysis (for example, if just one feature is chosen and simple linear regression is performed instead of multiple linear regression), the results can be misleading. This leaves the analyst vulnerable to any of various statistical paradoxes, or in some (not all) cases false causality as below.*

(Because the information on Wikipedia is open to editing, I have also included the references they used along with the Wikipedia link in notes.)[30][31][32]

All of this is important because government, healthcare, science, business, and social media enterprises collect and use data. The interpretation (and misinterpretation) of data can be used to help us or hurt us. Data can help businesses sell products and services. It can prove one drug to be more effective than another. It can be used politically to determine which policies to put into law or spend taxpayer dollars on. It can be used by your doctor to determine what medication to prescribe to you or what treatment to use for cancer, diabetes, and even COVID.[33]

If the data and subsequent assumptions about the data are inaccurate or misinterpreted, whether or not intentionally, it may hugely impact our lives. That helps us understand why one medical expert says masks protect us and another medical expert says masks can hurt us. There usually isn't just one single right way to address something. Additionally, information changes so fast that the information we have today may no longer apply tomorrow, as Dr. Siegel points out.

In this article, "Many Analysts, One Data Set: Making Transparent How Variations in Analytic Choices Affect Results," the author writes:

The observed results from analyzing a complex data set can be highly contingent on justifiable, but subjective, analytic decisions. Uncertainty in interpreting research results is therefore not just a function of statistical power or the use of questionable research practices; it is also a function of the many reasonable decisions that researchers must make in order to conduct the research.[34]

A physician friend told me that hormones are dangerous for women with a history of cancer. He backed up his position by quoting a particular study. Another physician friend told me that hormones were fine for women who've had cancer, and he backed it up with a different study. Who should I believe? Who is correct?

It depends on your point of view and the data you read and the interpretation the writer provided for that data and the credentials of the writer and your level of respect for that publication. In the graph with explanation shown below, the writer shows that the SAME information can be used to PROVE opposite "facts," depending on where you begin measuring.

Research Mindedness: Misuse of Research[35]

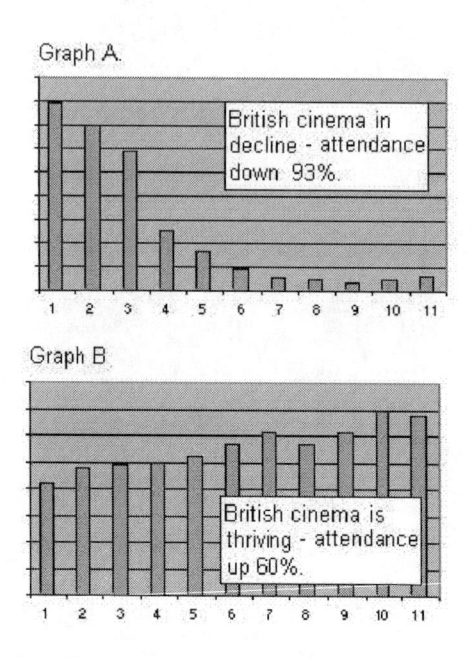

Graph A.

British cinema in decline - attendance down 93%.

Graph B.

British cinema is thriving - attendance up 60%.

Party politics thrive on the systematic use and misuse of research and monitoring data and are a rich arena for studying how the same information can be twisted to suit different ends. As with Graph B above, simply using different starting points (e.g., for inflation, unemployment, or crime figures—all of which might affect the public's moviegoing habits) can wholly change how figures are seen and the possible interpretations placed upon them.

Self-Persuasion

As I stated in the beginning of this chapter, this information is going to push your emotional buttons and that means it's pretty hard to digest. There's one last thing you need to understand about human beings and how the mind works: no one wants to be wrong. Why? Because it embarrasses us, makes us look and feel foolish, and has the potential to shake us to our core. If we've been fooled or proven wrong about something that we fully believed, then what else might we be wrong about? It makes us feel anxious and out of control, and we lose trust not only in the person who deceived us but also in ourselves and our ability to discern. If what we accepted as the truth is found to be wrong or, even worse, a lie, it creates internal discord and we immediately want to shut that down. If we prove to ourselves that we're right, then we can relax and comfortably go about our life.

It doesn't matter if we're talking about politics or spouses or parents or friends. If your best friend goes behind your back and uses what you told them against you or sleeps with your spouse, it rocks your world. Because you didn't see it coming. It took you by surprise. You were fooled. And that makes you doubt your judgment. And you become skeptical toward other people and other things that you took for granted. Once trust is shaken, almost everything gets viewed through a magnifying glass of hypervigilance. And inside you feel confused, disheartened, vulnerable, and distrustful.

No one wants to be in that position. That's why many people refuse to believe that their spouse is cheating, even when their best friend proves it to them. They reject the information because their inner mind cannot tolerate what it would mean. It's a form of survival response. So, instead, they get mad at the best friend. Why? Because believing it rocks the foundation of their beliefs and they can't tolerate that. As a marriage counselor and psychotherapist, I've heard countless stories from adults who were sexually abused in their youth by a family member or a family friend and when they told their own parent, they were scolded, punished, and shut down. When we're in a bind and we cannot comprehend the information, the mind blocks it. When we're frightened, we freeze or flee or block it.

Once a person decides which political side they align with, they tend to trust only that side and watch only that which supports their chosen political view. That means they're getting the same message, the same point of view, over and over and over. We become parrots of what we hear. Our chosen side is seen as credible and trustworthy so, of course, we believe what they feed us about the other side. Because we trust them, we feel little or no need to verify the data provided by them or their trusted resource. We accept blindly but receive shades of the truth, and as a result, our point of view narrows and our mind closes more and we hold tighter to our position.

When we're fed information that says that one person or one group is a danger to a person or a community or a nation, the survival instinct becomes activated. As a result, people will do what they feel they must do to protect themselves. And, unless we understand how it happens, why it happens, how to investigate the "facts," and how to soothe our own emotional state, we're all in big trouble. We will be easily led and manipulated into being participants in the demise of our precious world.

We need to understand and remember in the heat of the moment that the people who hold extreme positions are reactive because they are emotionally triggered and feel threatened or abandoned or violated in some way. Their emotions are being activated because someone or something is fanning the flames of fear. If we don't pay attention, history will repeat itself, making it OK to be intolerant of our differences. And once we make it OK to be intolerant of our differences, we lose compassion for people. That makes our thinking rigid and our behavior justified.

> Once we make it OK to be intolerant of our differences, we lose compassion for others. That makes our thinking rigid and our behavior justified.

We develop *group think* and we become a shell of who we truly are and who we are meant to be. We step into a zombie-like mindset. Remember, Jesus was hung on the cross for his beliefs. The Blacks were enslaved. The Jews were handed bars of soap and marched to gas chambers. All because of fears fed to the masses about their differences.

The Milgram experiment studied obedience. The study demonstrated that people will use their power against another person when they are told to do so and given the authority to do so. It proved easier when the person was out of sight, behind a wall. The study subjects thought they were part of an experiment about learning and memory. The subjects were placed in a position of authority and instructed to incrementally increase the voltage of painful electric shock to the learner when the learner answered incorrectly. The shock went from 30 volts up to 450 volts. The subject did not know that the machine didn't actually work and that only the dial moved. And the subject also did not know that the "learners" were actors who were just playing that role.

The degree of obedience was the highest when they weren't in the same room and they couldn't see the learners. They continued to follow the rules and obediently increased the shock up to 450 volts despite the screams from the learners or the banging on the wall or the learners begging the subject to stop.

Milgram believed that the reason the subjects continued to increase the shock was either because they believed they were inferior to the experimenter, whose orders they were following, or they were not responsible because they were following orders, or because the shock was minimal at first and slowly increasing incrementally. You can read more at the link shown in this note.[36]

Think about the similarity between the willingness to hurt someone from behind a wall and attacking someone on social media, from behind a computer. Isn't that what bullying looks like between school-age children? The amount of bullying has risen substantially with the use of social media.

Think about how many people you no longer speak with, mostly because they have opposing opinions about vaccines, masks, politics, worldviews, government policies, educational values, and stances on race and gender. This is evidence of the power of suggestion and the intentional use of emotion in pushing our buttons. What do you think will happen if we're repeatedly told by an authority that a person, a race, a religion, or anyone who thinks differently from us is dangerous? It's been shown that, over time, we will come to believe it. This is similar to the experiment above and history repeating itself.

With the onset of COVID, more Americans were diagnosed with an anxiety disorder. More people are having panic attacks. Alcoholism and obesity are on the rise. Overeating and excessive drinking are coping mechanisms and escape mechanisms people engage in and become trapped by when they are distressed and cannot find a way out. These behaviors are driven by fear and worry.

We're at an important fork in the road. We have to choose whether to be part of the problem and fan the flames of internal and external emotion, judgment, and chaos or choose to be part of the solution. To be part of the solution, we must learn how to calm our emotions so that we can see things clearly and then use our logical mind to move forward. Here are some ways to keep yourself grounded in difficult times.

1. **Center yourself.** The best thing you can do to combat the overload is to be intentional about what you listen to or watch, especially in the hour or two before bedtime. That's the time the mind is most easily influenced, because the messages we see and hear drop unfiltered as we near the very suggestible hypnagogic state, which you know is the state between awake and asleep. Turn off the news and, instead, take the time to bask in the good feelings you share with the special people and pets in your life. Remind yourself about the many ways you've been blessed. At bedtime I speak this prayer: Thank you, G-d, for your blessings and your favor. Thank you that good always overrides evil in me, in others, and in the world.

2. **Listen to uplifting messages.** There are tons of inspirational influencers, rabbis, pastors, motivators, neighbors, people we know, and people we've heard of who remind us that we

are strong and we have what it takes inside and that we are not alone. Joel Osteen has a wonderful way of bringing hope and peace to the mind and spirit. If you're spiritually based, you might tap into Laina Orlando, who teaches from A Course in Miracles perspective. Music can be an uplifting source of hope too. Find a support source that aligns with you.

3. **Notice what is joyful.** When we focus on the thoughts, feelings, and experiences that are joyful, we feel better. When we do this, the brain sends relaxation chemicals throughout our entire system, which strengthens the immune system, lifts our spirits, and feeds our soul. Begin a habit of noticing what's joyful in your life. Maybe it's a child, a parent, a spouse, a pet, a friend, a home, or even a beautiful plant. Create a daily habit of noticing that over what's bad.

4. **Imagine with intention.** Choose with intention how you use your imagination. As Dan Zadra, author and creativity consultant, tells us, "Worry is a misuse of the imagination." And Bruce Lipton, cell biologist and internationally recognized authority in bridging science and spirit, tells us that our thoughts don't just sit inside of our heads, their energy surrounds us and spills out into our world. Over the last 35 years, research by the World Peace

Project has shown that through the Radiance Effect, 53 meditation trials actually lowered crime, warfare, terrorism, and conflict across the world.[37] They had people envisioning world peace at a certain time of day all across the world. You can call it coincidence, but research shows it is something much more powerful and something that we can make use of.

5. **Don't give in to fear messages.** Remember, the brain is wired to pay attention when it perceives danger. Media experts, celebrities, and politicians know that and use fear to increase our allegiance and viewership. More viewers equal more money. The current structure of the news is designed to emphasize fear and worry messages and to make someone a villain. Keep that in mind when you hear the news. Knowing their plan returns your power to you.

6. **Exercise your compassion.** Remind yourself that when people's opinions are strong and rigid, it's usually because they've had traumatic experiences and the trauma center in their brain is likely being activated. What you're seeing is a survival response. People who've been hurt are more suggestible to messages around their pain than those who have not experienced something of that nature. If you get activated by their

emotional response and you respond in kind, all you're doing is fanning the fire. Instead, recognize that it's coming from a pain point and find compassion for them, just as you found compassion for both Person A and Person B in the drunk-driving scenario.

7. **Master your mind.** Most of us were not taught how to use our minds for our benefit, so we allow our mind to control us. That's because no one taught us that we don't have to be victims of every thought in our head. Dr. Daniel Amen recommends using ANT therapy, which teaches a person to question their Automatic Negative Thoughts. That's a very helpful exercise.

If you're interested in learning how to master your mind, register for the **Self-Hypnosis Workshop** or just book a free 15-minute phone consult to discuss the best options for reaching your goals. Find both at **www.LauraTemin.com**.

9

TRAUMA

The key to communication is listening.
—Dr. Jocelyn Elders

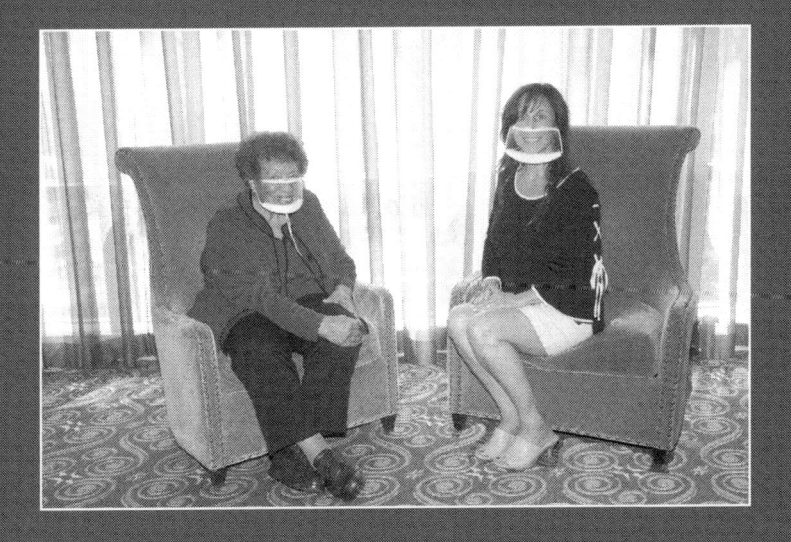

Jocelyn Elders, M.D., seen here with me, educator, pediatrician, 15th Surgeon General of the United States of America—the first woman and the first African American Surgeon General of the United States.

Dr. Elders understands the value of listening—listening to understand. Essentially, she knows that you cannot help a person if you don't understand the world they live in, their perspective, and what matters to them.

I suspect that trauma is part of every physician's life. The physical and emotional health of people are placed on their shoulders every day. They deal with the terminally ill, the chronically ill, the emotionally ill, and crisis situations. They're expected to quickly solve 20–30 complex puzzles every day, perfectly, despite hidden information, and they must address new puzzles every 15–20 minutes.

Now imagine multiplying that responsibility by millions. As the Surgeon General of the United States, Dr. Elders was the doctor for an entire nation. Her role was to address the most critical issues that plagued the nation, to lead and communicate directly with the public, and to guide 6,000 officers whose mission is to protect, promote, and advance the health of our nation.

During her term, AIDS was an epidemic, and she saw clearly that protecting the nation required openly discussing sex and drug use in an attempt to inform and educate about safe sex to avoid the transmission of this deadly disease. And what happened? She was forced to resign.

Trauma comes in many forms and has different degrees. In this chapter, you will understand what trauma really is and its impact on our lives.

Most people think of trauma as an outcome of a major catastrophic event. And it is. But trauma can also be subtle, like rainwater that seeps into cracks and crevices, drop by drop, over time, creating an infestation of mold. Trauma is actually anything that somehow shakes our foundation and alters a person's life. It creates a shift in thinking or in beliefs. And *trauma frequently follows drama.*

The majority of problems, habits, and addictions that I see result from what you might consider a small or insignificant incident. Something that you just can't seem to forget and you say, "Oh, it's nothing. It's typical kid stuff," or "It happens to everyone." You play it down because you were told that it's no big deal. Or you pushed it away or stuffed it down inside where it's just not consciously accessible. But it rattled you. That's the drama I'm referring to.

For nine years I worked in the emergency department in a hospital system. It was my job to evaluate the patients who were experiencing a severe crisis. They may have attempted suicide or threatened suicide. They may have been hearing voices or seeing things that no one else could see or hear. They may have been in an elevated, unpredictable, manic state. Or they may have been drunk, strung out, or in withdrawal. My job was to evaluate the person and determine what level of care they needed. Did they simply need to see a therapist to talk things out, or did they need to see a psychiatrist for medication? Were they safe to go home, or did they need hospitalization to become stabilized, or perhaps a medical detox?

I remember evaluating a woman who was taken by the police to the hospital because she told someone she was suicidal. If a person wants to kill themself, tries to kill themself, or has a plan to do so, they are considered "a danger to themself" and held in the hospital for evaluation so that they do not self-harm. They remain there until they're either accepted into a psychiatric hospital for stabilization or deemed to be stable enough to go home with an appointment for outpatient care.

The woman I was sent to evaluate was in her 70s. She was soft-spoken and very sad. She told me that her husband had dementia and had been in a nursing home for the past two years. That ate away all of their savings and put them in debt. Their house was foreclosed on, and every cent they had went to pay for his care. A month prior, he had passed away. They had no children. And at this point in time, she was homeless and she was tired. She had nothing left to live for, no place to stay, and she was ready to die.

She said she had lived her life. She said it was mostly a good life. But now everything had been stripped from her. She couldn't work. She had no job and no marketable skills. Her body wasn't strong, and she couldn't stand on her feet very long. She suspected she would be lucky to earn minimum wage, and she didn't want to live out the rest of her years just trying to survive.

She couldn't understand why the hospital was going to force her to stay alive. She couldn't understand how we could send her to a psychiatric hospital and let her mount up even more debt that she would not be able to pay. She just wanted to be left alone to handle her life or death as she saw fit.

This conversation made a huge impact on me. It was a simple, honest, painful conversation with a real person who questioned the role of the hospital in saving lives at all costs. I could certainly see her point. I thought about how I might feel if I were she. Would I want to live in some shelter, or would I want to quietly leave the earth? Why is it that a system gets to decide the fate of a person at that person's personal, spiritual, physical, or financial expense, without giving that person a say in the matter? That experience shook me.

As an employee of that hospital, and under the ethical guidelines of my license, I was obligated to protect her life and recommend to the physician who ultimately made all decisions that she be sent to a psychiatric hospital because she was a danger to herself. And I had to grapple with the horrible consequences this decision would surely create for this woman. I knew that sending her to a psychiatric hospital would rack up more expenses for her, which was one of the elements that caused her to feel suicidal.

Yet on the other hand, *what if* just around the corner, there was some unforeseen miracle that awaited her? Maybe at the psychiatric hospital she would meet a youngster who had tried to take her own life because her mother had passed away and they immediately connected. And *what if* the father, who was suddenly a single parent, was in desperate need of a live-in nanny who understood his daughter and he offered this woman a job, a place to live, and a purpose? Miracles happen.

TRAUMA FOLLOWS DRAMA

Think about a child who was bullied, or a child who stood before the class, making a presentation with food stuck in their tooth or snot in their nose as children pointed and laughed, but that child had no idea why they were laughing. Think about a person whose spouse cheated on them and how that might make them feel. Think about a kid whose parent is verbally unkind whenever that parent drinks, and says the most hurtful words.

> Trauma can be subtle, like rainwater that seeps into cracks, drop by drop, over time, creating an infestation of mold.

Trauma follows drama, and they piggyback onto other fear experiences and create or strengthen those beliefs. What I've described may not be the same kind of trauma as having a gun in your face, but they're subtle and significant experiences. And they have the potential to change beliefs and attach to other beliefs. This is what I'm calling *subtle, significant internalized trauma,* like my hospital experience, which made me question both sides of blanket policies and shifted my perspective, my automatic response to diagnoses, labels, charges, and accusations, even the labels that once had no wiggle room such as sex offender, addict, cheater.

If you're having a visceral reaction to that statement, I don't blame you. I would also, if I had never had the experiences that I had had in the hospital emergency room or in my role doing drug and alcohol evaluations for the state or working with so-called multiple offenders in juvenile court.

What comes to mind when you hear the label "multiple offender" in juvenile court? My mind pulled up a picture of kids who had no conscience. Vicious, dangerous, angry kids. Sociopathic kids. Troublemakers. And since I was providing an Anger Management program, I assumed they were all filled with anger. And it got worse once I saw the charges, which included "sex offender." That sent chills up my spine. The label fed my imagination with brutal sexual acts. Things I'd see on the news or in horror movies.

But when I actually read the charts, I saw that the sex offender label was assigned when a boy threw candy down a classmate's shirt. And when I met the boy and saw this chubby, socially awkward, kid, I thought I had the wrong chart or the wrong boy. And when I heard his story, I understood *how* he was given the label and the wide range of actions that might cause a person to be labeled as a sex offender. But in the end, that act of throwing the candy down her shirt and attempting to reach in to get it is considered a sexual offense. But when you see the label "sex offender," do you ask what happened? Most people make assumptions—and not for the best. Completely understandable.

In a chart, the label reads one way. But face to face, it looks different. What I saw was an extremely immature 14-year-old boy. A boy who acted without thinking and paid dearly for it. But the rules are the rules. And what is inappropriate is inappropriate. And the deeply unfortunate thing is that labels, legal charges, and the shame of it follow us forward. Once the "yes" box is checked for legal history, most employers throw away the job application.

But my experience did not end there. I evaluated many people who were picked up by the sheriff's deputies because their spouse *claimed* that person had said they were going to kill themselves. All you have to do is call 911 and make that allegation against anyone, and they are immediately picked up and taken to the ER. It doesn't even have to be true. And often, behind the claim is a pending divorce and a spouse who is trying to build a custody case. The experience with the suicidal woman and the 14-year-old boy and the false accusation against an innocent person was a big trauma for them, and a subtle but significant internal trauma for me.

I came to realize that when a person has been given a label, and we don't know the person well, or the facts, we are actually reacting to our imagination or our experience of what the label represents to us. And then *we accept the label as a fact and as the sole truth and the door is sealed closed.* We don't even realize that's what we're doing, and we rarely look beneath the label or question ourselves. When a doctor, a clinician, or a judge assigns the label, and the news reports the label, followed by someone we trust or admire sharing the story, then we take that label as fact. Trauma follows drama.

Leah was a pretty little girl who loved attention. She was outgoing and friendly and treasured dressing up. Her favorite clothes were girly, ruffled dresses. And she decided to wear them to school with her shiny patent leather shoes. The first time she wore her yellow party dress to school, some of the girls teased and made fun of her. But she felt like a princess when she dressed up, so she didn't care what they said and she wore another party dress the next day. The reactions from the other girls were even more ugly. They called her "show-off" and "big shot" and told her that she was ugly and her dresses were ugly. They tugged at her bows with dirty hands and pulled them out of shape. As adults, we can see through that. But as kids, we can't. We all want to be accepted and loved. When our friends, teachers, or classmates shame or humiliate us, we feel rejected, judged, unsafe, and insecure. It makes us second-guess ourselves. It makes us shrink. We want to hide or run away and we'll do anything to make it stop, even if it means backing down, giving in, or suffocating our authentic self in order to fit in.

Remember, when we're young, we have no filter, no analyzing ability, and no experience to put things in perspective; so, the things those other children and adults say to us can be accepted without question. Leah followed her parents' advice and tried to ignore it. When that didn't work, she followed their next suggestion to stand up for herself, but the girls came at her with a vengeance. They pushed her down and took scissors to her dress and chopped off her beautiful ruffles. And that was the end of Princess Leah.

Less than a week later, the pretty party dresses were shoved out of sight, into the back of the closet. She no longer wore them to school. She no longer wore them to church. The joy of stepping into the magical princess experience lasted only a few weeks, but the drama and trauma sent the princess into hiding. It changed her self-view, her worldview, and the course of her life. And it remained in her mind in detail for decades.

At 56 years old, Leah came to see me. She said she wanted to lose weight and feel less anxious. As we spoke, I learned more about her eating habits and what drove them. I learned more about her anxious feelings and when they were triggered. She spoke about a sense of panic and doom whenever she had to be assertive and stand up for herself. She felt frozen, like a little girl, and she couldn't get the words out. She told me about the business she owned and the discomfort she felt at being in the spotlight. She told me about being fat and the countless diets that never worked. She said that all she hoped for at that moment was to be able to accept herself as a fat person and love herself in that body, since it was clear to her that being fat would never change. She said that she knew what to eat and how to eat, but she just couldn't seem to do it. And she shared the details of that earlier experience.

> Traumatic events cause a person to enter a hypnotic state. Trauma follows drama.

Trauma follows drama. Leah knew the experience played a role in her life, but she couldn't figure out what or why or how to fix it. She understood that it was a long time ago. She had even worked through the experience with a therapist. But the feelings lingered. The event left an indelible mark in her mind and still influenced her thoughts, feelings, and actions. This event was not a horrible plane crash or car accident. No one died. But a part of her did.

When I asked what meaning she made from the event, she said, "It's better not to look too good, and certainly not to stand out, because people can be vicious." She was afraid to stand up for herself because there were always repercussions. She understood it. She knew where it came from and even stated that, logically, she thought it was ridiculous because it had happened so long ago. This is an example of trauma following drama. I know that if a problem, the interpretation, and the feelings are alive in the subconscious mind, that means all the logic in the world won't change it. It needs to be resolved through the subconscious mind. You can try to reason with emotions, but you won't get anywhere.

Trauma and Hypnosis

Dr. Jean-Martin Charcot (1825–1893), a French neurologist, was the first to connect hysteria and trauma to the hypnotic state. He recognized that traumatic events cause a person to enter a hypnotic state. He identified the dissociative aspect and the suggestibility aspect.

When a person dissociates, they are physically present but they are removed. You can see when a person is dissociating because they have that blank stare or faraway look on their face, which we commonly call *zoning out*. They are looking through us or past us even though their eyes are focused on us. In fact, they might even be nodding their head as we speak, but the faraway look in their eyes reflect the state. The trance state is the go-to state for the mind in the midst of trauma. And you already know that it is also the go-to state when we are tired or overwhelmed.

Look at the photo of these two children, and you can clearly see that the child on the right is in a trance state and the other child isn't. This trance state may last only a few moments, and we move in and out of that state every day, many times a day. Being in a trance state doesn't mean that a person is experiencing trauma, but a person who is experiencing trauma usually dissociates and enters a trance state.

ACCIDENTAL HYPNOSIS

Below is another example of the difference between the actively engaged state and the trance state.

39 40

The best definition of *dissociation* I've found is on Wikipedia. It is a compilation from a variety of sources, as you can see from my link below and in the references I copied from their site (see notes):

> Dissociation is commonly displayed on a continuum. In mild cases, dissociation can be regarded as a coping mechanism or defense mechanism in seeking to master, minimize or tolerate stress—including boredom or conflict. At the non-pathological end of the continuum, dissociation describes common events such as daydreaming. Further along the continuum are non-pathological altered states of consciousness.[41]

When we face unbearable events, things we can't make sense of or something intolerable, we escape by dissociating ... disconnecting, disengaging. Violence, physical and sexual abuse, and witnessing or being part of catastrophic events are some examples of severe trauma. But it's important to note that the severity of the event is *not the only* determinant of the degree of trauma. A person's coping ability, level of emotional stability, and degree of resiliency *at that moment in time* plays a significant role. We're less resilient after a series of stressful life events than we are when life is comfortably rolling along. If we had a cold followed by a fender bender, and before that we had nursed our aging family dog, we'll have less emotional stamina than we would after a fun vacation.

Because traumatic events are emotionally intense, they activate the limbic system, our emotional brain. Extreme distress and fear quickly produce a hyper-suggestible state. Scientifically speaking, because traumatic events tap into the limbic system, they have the potential to shut down or limit access to the logical part of the brain and our ability to formulate words. So, essentially, we stand there open-mouthed, in shock, dissociating, and in a trance. Doesn't that sound like what Leah was describing when she was bullied? Isn't that what happens when we're in shock or in danger? We feel stuck and stifled and speechless.

Here's what Bessel van der Kolk, M.D., says in his book *The Body Keeps the Score*:[42]

> *Traumatized people become stuck, stopped in their growth because they can't integrate new experiences into their lives ... Being traumatized means continuing to organize your life as if the trauma were still going on—unchanged and immutable—as every new encounter or event is contaminated by the past.*

This may seem extreme to some people and for some situations, depending on a person's degree of resiliency. Some people who are more resilient may not experience a traumatic response or may be able to cope with it better than those who are less resilient. But for many people and many situations it's exactly as Dr. van der Kolk describes, and it is certainly not a one-and-done experience. It's an experience that leaves us with a message. That message is internalized and carried forward and becomes part of who we are and how we see the world.

Can you see the relationship to Accidental Hypnosis? That's why it's so important for you to understand how Accidental Hypnosis works and what it is, because when you understand what creates the state, you can take steps to prevent yourself from being emotionally hijacked.

Setting the Stage — Parental Relationships

You may have heard the old saying "Sticks and stones may break my bones, but words can never harm me."

Actually, that's not exactly true. As you have seen, words have tremendous power. The words you say, the words you hear, and the words you repeat to yourself can hurt you. They may not physically break your bones, but they have the potential for damage that lasts a lifetime.

When we're young, we don't fully understand words or the meaning behind them, so we rely heavily on the nonverbal cues and the feelings they stir. We interpret facial expressions, body language, tone, volume, and intensity. But because our understanding and life experience are limited, we may misread what is said or meant.

The parent-child relationship is a person's first and most important relationship. It typically sets the relationship tone for a lifetime. When a parent betrays a child's trust, abandons them in some way, physically hurts, shames, or embarrasses them, it has the potential to severely impact that child—not only in that moment but well into the future. Children depend on their parents for protection and survival. They may not be consciously aware that their survival is dependent on their caregiver until their foundation is rocked. When that happens, it sends a kind of electric shock to the child and even young children wonder, "What will happen to me?" An example of this is when there is a divorce. Many children worry about what will happen to them. Who will they live with? How will their world change?

ACCIDENTAL HYPNOSIS

Just as we saw with Zelda, children can only sort things out based on their own experiences and their own limited thinking. The words parents speak, the tone they use, their body language and behavior are exaggerated in the child's mind, especially when the parent and child are visibly upset. Just like adults, children give meaning to experiences in their own limited way, based primarily on feelings and assumptions. Their interpretations aren't well filtered because of their heightened emotions and their limited experiences, so the mind accepts the interpretation as fact and as truth, and those misinterpretations can easily become a foundational, core belief.

If a child can't count on their parent or caregiver for stability or protection, they get the message, "I'm not safe," or "I'm all alone." They may believe "I'm not loveable," "I'm defective," or "No one loves me." Those messages travel forward with them. The message may be true in that moment regarding that parent or specific to that situation. Or it may be untrue and misread. But the child is unable to make those distinctions. Even as adults, we're constantly reading situations and their intended meanings, and there's so much room for misinterpretation because we're processing everything through our own mind and our past experiences.

You already know that our decisions about the meaning of something can be made in a flash, and whether we're a child or an adult, such interpretations are rarely ever questioned or reviewed afterward. Those inaccurate interpretations become beliefs, and those beliefs become generalized, spreading into other areas of our lives. That's why a child with an abusive father may feel uncomfortable about sharing a different opinion with his male boss, because his mind associates the same threat of danger with all authority figures, particularly men. If his dad wore glasses or had his arms folded or was drinking scotch when he was being abusive, then it's not unusual for the subconscious mind to feel fear or discomfort in the face of any or all of those elements.

> The parental and spousal relationships are the most influential relationships in our lives.

Everything we see, hear, and experience is logged in the inner mind, and much of it is also stored in the body. But we do not realize it. So much happens on the subconscious level because the subconscious mind is always awake and always monitoring everything. It's the subconscious mind that forms the beliefs, holds the memories, and therefore, tells the conscious mind whether to date again, trust again, diet again, and anything else; yet we remain blind to it.

I believe that everyone gets stuck, to some degree, in some area at some point, and everyone carries some degree of the past forward. We all have a past, and we all have perceptions, interpretations, and misinterpretations. We have trouble seeing the connections in relation to ourselves because we live in our own heads, and there's no distance, so there's no perspective. Essentially, we operate within our own blind spots. Just like Michael's one incident with Mandy became a generalization he applied to all women, each of us drags elements from our past into the future to some degree.

The subconscious mind stores the experience in the mind and often in the body as well. As a result, we might wind up with chronic headaches, digestive problems, sexual problems, fibromyalgia, cancer, panic attacks, depression, or anxiety. We might turn to drugs or alcohol or some other numbing agent when we cannot break free of our limiting beliefs or release the past or manage a current situation.

As stated earlier, the parental and spousal relationships are the most influential relationships in our lives. If the people with whom we have our most-trusted relationships betray us in a significant way, whether the betrayal is real or imagined, it has a ripple effect in many areas of our lives.

43

Look at the photo above. What do you see? What's the story in your mind about this photo? Can you feel the intensity? Is your mind imagining the loud shrieking sound of the woman's voice or perhaps the smell of her breath? Or are you seeing a boy whose mother is leaning in and he is just closing down and turning away? Are you having a physical or emotional reaction? The degree to which you experience those feelings speaks volumes about your degree of suggestibility at this moment or its relationship to your past or the present.

Everything you see gets processed through your own mind. And we are most sensitive to that which we have experienced.

If you'd like to peek further into your mind and possibly tap into some hidden beliefs that might have some degree of control over you, read the exercise questions as you look

ACCIDENTAL HYPNOSIS

at the photos below. It's a self-exploration exercise which might provide insight into your worldview, your self-view, or the dominant message you carry inside. You don't have to share your interpretation of the photos with anyone, but see if there is a theme. Also, notice that faraway look in the photos, so when you see the trance state in real life, you will recognize it for what it is.

Exercise:

1. What are you feeling?
2. What's the story?
3. What's the message?

Exercise:

1. What are you feeling?
2. What's the story?
3. What's the message?

Exercise:

1. What are you feeling?
2. What's the story?
3. What's the message?

Exercise:

1. What are you feeling?
2. What's the story?
3. What's the message?

Exercise:

1. What are you feeling?
2. What's the story?
3. What's the message?

One thing I can say with certainty is that your mind wants to release the conflicts and burdens you carry, and the mind has the ability to do that and turn your life around. You just have to give it what it needs to make that happen.

I've seen people with long-standing addictions turn things around. I've seen people haunted by the memory of infidelity release the pain of the past and love again. I've seen people forgive themselves and others for things they believed were unforgivable and positively change the course of their lives.

Your mind wants to be free of the weight of the past, the regrets, the hurts, the mistakes you made, and the mistakes made against you. Your mind even wants to release the pain of unforgivable acts, whether you were on the giving or receiving end. It wants to make sense of the hurts and resolve them so you can let them go. It just doesn't know how, or it would. It's time to learn how it's done.

CONCLUSION

Endings and New Beginnings

Whatever we plant in our subconscious mind and nourish with repetition and emotion will one day become a reality.
—Earl Nightingale

LAURA TEMIN

That's the truth! Unfortunately, most of us are unaware of the power we have and what we set in motion. Hindsight is always 20/20. Travel down memory lane with me, and I'll share the details of my story and how this concept played out in my life. It happened in plain sight, without any awareness on my part. I didn't know then what I know now, but looking back, I can see how all the elements were in play.

> In the heightened state of an aha moment, feelings are cemented and instructions are given to the subconscious mind to be carried out.

I was a budding artist. I loved to draw and I loved to sculpt. I was thrilled that I was accepted into the High School of Music and Art. I lived in Queens and the school was in Manhattan. I was even willing to travel an hour-plus, by subway, just get to and from school.

Every morning, I rode the train during rush hour. That means I squeezed into the packed train like a sardine and stood smashed against stinky armpits of stoic grownups. No one looking at anyone. Everyone scrambling for a seat or a place their hand could hold onto the steel pole. But what stood out to me, above it all, was the look on the faces of the adults who were headed to work. The frown marks were seared into their brows. Their mouths turned down into a grimace. They looked worn and hollow. It was a familiar look I'd seen on the faces of the adults in my neighborhood, in my building and, to some degree, even my father.

He told me more than once, "Bosses don't care about you. They only care about themselves." I didn't understand at that age that what he was really saying was that he was frustrated and unhappy with his job and he felt stuck. That he had to work to support his family, and he was disappointed and hopeless. This was not the way he was told it would be. And he had to accept it. And he wanted me to know what to expect.

At some point, as I rode that train, it dawned on me that I was going to be working one day too, and that I, too, would be miserable just like everyone else. And in that aha moment, I took a vow that *I would never become that person!* I told myself, *If I am going to work for a living, I will do the kind of work that I love!*

Every day we make decisions. I didn't realize the power of that decision. I hadn't yet learned about the subconscious mind, and I certainly didn't realize that what I had actually done in that aha moment was provide instructions to my subconscious mind that were to be carried out. But that's exactly what I did. And you remember that intense emotion strengthens suggestions.

As I look back, I can see the relationship between that Earl Nightingale quote and my first career, my current career, my marriage, finding my first dog and every dog, and even the connection with my mentors. Everything is connected. And it all begins in the mind.

To help you see how my subconscious mind took the lead, and how I fed my subconscious mind, let me share my senior year in college.

My major was fine art. My minor was psychology. I loved to think. I loved to explore the mind, but I loved art even more. I was about to graduate but I still had no idea of how I was going to make a living. One thing I knew for sure was that I wanted to do work that I loved. The question was, *How would I make a living doing art?* I had no idea. But as Earl Nightingale's quote essentially states, when a thought, a dream, a wish is held fiercely in the mind and emotionally fed, it takes on a life of its own and becomes a reality. Here's what happened.

One night, my sister and I were walking into a restaurant. She noticed two men who were about to leave. She said to me, "These guys look like jewelers. I have some rings I want to sell. I'm going to talk to them." I thought she was nuts. What do jewelers look like? They were just two middle-aged men. We walked over to them and to my surprise, they were jewelers! They told us a story about two sisters who studied at the Fashion Institute of Technology in Manhattan and learned jewelry making and then opened a jewelry store. Was that a coincidence? Perhaps you might call it that. That's what I thought at the time. But today, I know it wasn't that at all. Today, I believe it was the subconscious mind merging with my deepest desires and G-d and the Universe lining things up for me.

Meeting those men, and hearing the story they told about the sisters, immediately provided a solution to my problem. It opened a door that I never could have seen. And that solution immediately excited me; it gave me a direction, and it offered me hope. That day led me on the path to my first career in the jewelry industry. Little by little, all the pieces continued coming together. Somehow the right people showed up at the right time, and it all unfolded very naturally.

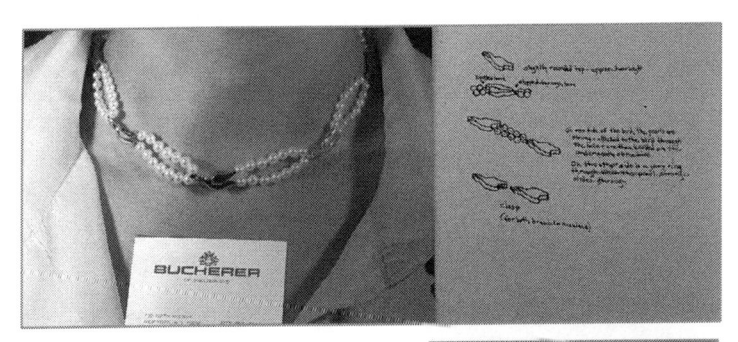

Once I was clear about my career, I set my sights on becoming a famous jewelry designer. My heart and mind were passionately set.

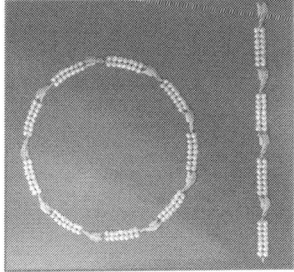

Although I never attained the kind of fame I had dreamed of, I can tell you that I reached my potential in that industry. My jewelry designs were fabricated and sold in many well-known stores across the country, and even in Switzerland. And that chapter led to the next. One thing always leads to the next. And we are meant to learn and build on every experience.

Most of us believe that once we find our path and put in the hard work and climb the ladder of success, we've paid our dues and we should be able to relax and coast for the rest of our lives, living comfortably, happily ever after. That's not the way it works.

We're meant to learn and grow. When we reach one goal, or when we are no longer excited by that goal, or when we need to develop new skills, we're pushed forward. But we enjoy the trappings of what is known. And we fight against the unknown. Yet when it is time to move on, we are forced to do so, or we will wind up living as a shell of who we really are and what we are meant to do and have and be.

Everything in my path was showing me that it was time to leave the jewelry industry. But I liked being comfortable. So, I pushed that growing feeling of boredom and dissatisfaction away. I had no idea of what I wanted to do next and I was afraid to let go of the security and comfort of what I had worked so hard for. Isn't that the truth that most of us struggle against?

ACCIDENTAL HYPNOSIS

*Too many of us are not living our dreams
because we are living our fears.*
—Les Brown

When it's time to change, the Universe gives us a nudge. If we ignore it, we get a shove. If we ignore that, we get clobbered. That's how it works.

The jewelry industry was changing. Customers were complaining and businesses were closing. It wasn't fun anymore. It took three gunpoint-robberies for me to get the message that I had better move on. I no longer loved my work. (Remember my vow to myself?) And my beautiful dream was becoming a nightmare.

I moved from New York to Georgia, hoping a change of address would make the difference. But fate follows us—or is it the subconscious mind driving things? Within two months of my move, I experienced another attempted robbery. And that was the hit that took me out of the game. I remember wanting to leave the industry after the second robbery, but I knew that it would negatively impact my partner, and I had a moral obligation to him. He needed me, just as I needed him. And he was my friend. I remember telling myself and him that day that if it happened one more time, I would leave with a clear conscience.

That third attempt left me so severely traumatized, not only could I not work, but I couldn't even get myself to leave my home. My role in our business was sales. My partner handled everything inside. And he was as patient as anyone could be, hoping I would shake off the fear and get back out there again. But I was frozen. Immobilized. And if I couldn't do my job, what value did I bring to our partnership? Finally, after several fruitless months, that chapter ended.

"Everything that happens to us, happens for us." I don't know who said this, and at that time, I surely didn't believe that having a gun pointed in my face and experiencing severe financial losses and near-death experiences could ever remotely be considered "for me." But today, I see it differently.

Although I no longer loved the jewelry industry, I still loved seeing my favorite customers. I loved being around beautiful jewelry. I loved working with my partner and his family. And I loved that we took a chance and we made our dream come true. Not all the way, but we crossed the finish line.

Yet, there I sat, afraid to leave home. I knew in my heart that my career was over. I had no idea how I'd support myself. But what I had been doing was no longer possible for me. I had no interest in starting all over again. I was in no position for that. I was divorced. I had just moved to a new state. I was alone and scared and confused. But when it's over, it's over, and all that's left is to take the next step.

ACCIDENTAL HYPNOSIS

> It's never too late to be what
> you might have been.
> —George Eliot

At this writing, I have been in this career for 23 years. I absolutely love what I do. But that doesn't mean things went smoothly or that I've reached all my goals ... yet. I'm still a work in progress. I'm still being pushed and forced to grow and change. It's not comfortable. It's not easy. But the rewards are many.

I'm here to tell you that what you want is possible for you. It requires a shift into curiosity. To get there, you must refuse to look for evidence that you'll never have what you want. Instead, eagerly look for clues that reveal who or what belief stands in the way. Take out a magnifying glass and trace those beliefs back to the source. The people, the patterns, the interpretations, the stories, the lies, the misunderstandings, the aha moments that contributed to the belief that's still holding you hostage.

And then, with an open mind, question which of your beliefs belong in the past, and whether they are worth holding onto. And lastly, decide to turn things around by building a new belief and, through hindsight, seek evidence that supports it.

The gap between where you are and where you want to be can narrow and disappear. What once seemed unattainable, impossible, unresolvable, no longer has to be.

The first step of solving any problem or reaching any goal is getting clear about what the problem or goal is. Use the free tools available to you that I've mentioned throughout the book to help you unveil the beliefs that are controlling and shortchanging your life.

1. Begin by choosing one area in which you have an ongoing problem.
   For example: relationship problems.
2. Look for the belief that you have around this ongoing problem.
   For example: men/women are not trustworthy.
3. Look for the events or people who created or reinforced the belief.
   For example: a parent who cheated or people you dated who cheated or someone you love who was hurt by an unfaithful partner.
4. Look for the messages you heard, accepted, or gave yourself around this problem.
   For example: "Why bother dating, all the good ones are taken," or "Only the cheaters are left," or "I'm destined to be alone."

The next step is to give your subconscious mind a new message.

A. BUILD AWARENESS

1. Look for evidence that your old, limiting belief is not 100 percent accurate. For example, think of all the couples you know who are loyal and trustworthy to their partner/spouse.

B. ACTION STEPS

1. Write down the new message you want to give yourself. For example: "There are millions of people who want a loving and committed relationship and they are looking for me. I am a magnet for forever love."
2. Before bed, imagine the feeling of being in a committed loving relationship with someone who feels like you were the answer to their prayers. And bask in the feeling. Then give yourself the suggestion that you have written.
3. Write it nightly. Repeat it nightly. Bask in the feeling/vision nightly. You're using the Laws of Attraction, Association, and Repetition combined with the natural trance state to create a new belief.
4. Throughout the day take note of more and more evidence you find that supports your new belief and write that down as well.

Some problems are resolved easily, and for some you need an outside source to help you sort it through and dismantle what's no longer beneficial. Our Self-Hypnosis Mastery Workshop has stellar reviews and is an affordable place to begin. You'll gain greater insight and develop a valuable skill.

A Dose of Prevention

Now that you understand what Accidental Hypnosis is, how the mind works, and how beliefs form, you're in a much better position to prevent yourself from falling victim to Accidental Hypnosis in the future. Here's how:

1. Notice when you are overly tired or when you are dealing with a lot of stress. Remind yourself that this can put you in a highly suggestible state, so avoid watching scary shows, listening to the news, or talking to people who are problem-focused.

2. Refuse to think about upsets when you are in a suggestible state. Instead think about the people and things that fill your heart and make you smile.

3. Use the suggestible state to reinforce your goals.

4. Remember, with awareness, you have the ability to question your interpretations and block false beliefs before they are set.

5. Share what you've learned with everyone you know and love, so they can prevent themselves

from being controlled by their mind or the goals and beliefs of others. And everything you teach solidifies your understanding and retention.

Hypnotherapy is one of the gentlest and most respectful ways to soothe the emotions and align the conscious and subconscious mind, so that you can put things in perspective and move forward.

You Can't Keep a Good Dream Down

Your dreams have more power than you know. You may think of them as little annoyances, reminding you of what you're missing, but the truth is that all of your hopes, dreams, and desires—the ones that fill your heart, that keep resurfacing even though you keep pushing them down—are an intrinsic part of who you are and what you are meant to have. They're inside of you because they're meant to be fulfilled.

Of course you will have doubts and fears. But know that the dreams you are meant to act on will keep surfacing, because that driving force can't be held back. And those dreams are meant to be realized.

That's what I want for you: that your most precious dreams come true. And I know it is possible.

> *Most great people have attained their greatest success just one step beyond their greatest failure.*
> —Napoleon Hill

Do you remember the story of Humpty Dumpty? The nursery rhyme tells that he was an egg that fell off a wall and cracked. It says that none of the experts could put Humpty Dumpty back together again.

As you can see from the photo, Humpty Dumpty found someone who knew how to help, and he got a second chance. Now his future is bright.

Don't let other people's limiting beliefs dictate your future. Take your power back. A bright future is calling you!

NOW IS THE PERFECT TIME.

It's always impossible, until it's done.

—Nelson Mandela

RESOURCES

Sometimes we get everything we need from a book. Other times, reading the book readies us for the next step.

Personal Resources

If you have questions, you're welcome to schedule a complimentary 15-minute phone consultation. Go to www.Laura-Temin.com and schedule a call.

Professional Resources

There is no greater satisfaction than helping someone reach their goals. If you enjoy helping others and you're looking for a rewarding career where you can make a difference, be your own boss, and feel valued at any age and earn money, you might want to consider certification. The people who make the best hypnotherapists are the people who've experienced hardships, because it leaves us the gift of wisdom, greater insight, and compassion. More coaches, counselors, therapists, psychologists, teachers, veterans, retirees, and high school graduates are pursuing a career that gives them the freedom to live life on their terms and make a difference. Professional Hypnosis Institute is the only state-authorized school of Clinical Hypnosis in Georgia. Twenty-three years ago, my mentor had a vision and, despite a debilitating illness and her failing health, she held tight to her dream, and the school became a reality. I was one of her first students. Today, you can still become certified in Clinical, Medical, and Integrative Hypnosis with specialty training in Addictions, Relationships, Trauma, Weight Loss, and Sleep. (**www.Hypnotherapy.SCHOOL**)

Programs and Seminars

We offer an assortment of programs and seminars. To see our current classes, specials, and trainings, explore our website, send an email, or **schedule a 15-minute phone consult at: www.LauraTemin.com**

When you become the master of your mind,
you are master of everything.

—Swami Satchidananda

THE LAWS OF HYPNOSIS

Law of Repetition – The more we repeat something or hear it repeated or see it or experience it, the more automatic the idea becomes. We learn through repetition; after a while it becomes familiar, and what's familiar becomes accepted.

Law of Association – This law builds a connection between things that are not related so that when you think of one, you think of the other.

Law of Dominance – Examples of dominance in this sense are raising the volume, altering the speed, emphasizing or minimizing certain words, changing the tone, or using nonverbal cues such as facial expressions or a stance/pose. All of this may be used to increase the power of the message.

Law of Delayed Action – Suggestions can be acted upon immediately, or they may accumulate in the mind before we respond to them. Delayed reactions are an example of the Law of Delayed Action. It takes a triggering event to activate this suggestion.

Endnotes

1. https://pixabay.com/illustrations/hunger-meal-hungry-comic-food-not-4291379/
2. https://www.psychologytoday.com/us/basics/imposter-syndrome
3. https://www.mayoclinicproceedings.org/article/S0025-6196(11)63203-5/fulltext
4. https://pubmed.ncbi.nlm.nih.gov/21617788/ Magy Onkol. 2011 Mar;55(1):22-31.Epub 2011 Mar 31.[Possibilities of hypnosis and hypnosuggestive methods in oncology]
5. https://pubmed.ncbi.nlm.nih.gov/20576592/ Role of hypnosis and hypno-suggestions methods in the complex therapy of tumor patients
6. www.pixabay.com

7 https://staff.washington.edu/eloftus/Articles/sciam.htm

8 https://www.healthline.com/health/false-memory#why-we-have-them

9 https://en.wikipedia.org/wiki/Stimulus_(psychology)#/media/File:Pavlov's_dog_conditioning.svg

"File:Pavlov's dog conditioning.svg" by Maxxl[2] is licensed under CC BY-SA 4.0 "File:Pavlov's dog conditioning.svg" by Maxxl[2] is licensed under CC BY-SA 4.0 By Maxxl[2] - Own work - vectorizedPavlov dogs conditioning, CC BY-SA 4.0, https://commons.wikimedia.org/w/index.php?curid=32037734

https://creativecommons.org/licenses/by-sa/4.0/

10 https://pixabay.com/users/withromli-23314843/

11 https://atlantajewishtimes.timesofisrael.com/therapist-puts-new-face-on-alcoholism/

12 https://pubs.niaaa.nih.gov/publications/AA77/AA77.htm

13 https://www.cnn.com/2019/10/16/health/children-fruit-drinks-report-wellness/index.html

14 Photo by Criativithy from Pexels

15 www.abcnews.go.com/Health/teens-vulnerable-junk-food-advertising-experts/story?id=69060220

16 https://pixabay.com/users/conmongt-1226108 Image by Christian Dorn

17 http://uconnruddcenter.org/food-marketing
https://ijbnpa.biomedcentral.com/articles/10.1186/1479-5868-1-3

18 https://www.frontiersin.org/articles/10.3389/fnut.2021.645349/full

19 https://www.frontiersin.org/articles/10.3389/fnut.2021.645349/full

20 https://www.health.com/food/16-most-misleading-food-labels

21 https://c2.staticflickr.com/8/7402/8724241011_2b07be5b5b_b.jpg

22 https://smartlabel.hersheys.com/00034000140602-0010#ingredients

23 https://www.healthline.com/nutrition/too-much-sugar

https://www.healthline.com/nutrition/dark-chocolate-buyers-guide#TOC_TITLE_HDR_8

24 https://www.heart.org/en/healthy-living/healthy-eating/eat-smart/sugar/how-much-sugar-is-too-much

25 https://smartlabel.hersheys.com/00034000134625-0012#ingredients

26 https://www.healthline.com/health/sugar/healthline-survey-results#Breaking-up-is-hard-to-do

27 https://www.investopedia.com/managing-wealth/worth-playing-lottery/

28 https://www.scie.org.uk/publications/ researchmindedness/makingsenseofresearch/ misuseofresearch/

https://www.heritage.org/report/ un-data-and-statistics-manipulated-higher-purpose

29 Photo by Anton Uniqueton from Pexels

30 https://en.wikipedia.org/wiki/ Misuse_of_statistics#Misuse_of_ statistics#CITEREFSpirerSpirerJaffe1998

31 Spirer, Herbert; Spirer, Louise; Jaffe, A. J. (1998). Misused Statistics (revised and expanded 2nd ed.). New York: M. Dekker.
The book is based on several hundred examples of misuse.

32 Gardenier, John; Resnik, David (2002). "The misuse of statistics: concepts, tools, and a research agenda". Accountability in Research: Policies and Quality Assurance. 9 (2): 65–74. doi:10.1080/08989620212968. PMID 12625352. S2CID 24167609.

33 https://www.heritage.org/report/ un-data-and-statistics-manipulated-higher-purpose

34 https://journals.sagepub.com/ doi/10.1177/2515245917747646

35 https://www.scie.org.uk/publications/ researchmindedness/makingsenseofresearch/ misuseofresearch/

36 https://www.britannica.com/biography/ Stanley-Milgram

37 https://www.worldpeacegroup.org/world_peace_research.html
38 Photo by Eren Li from Pexels
39 www.pexels.com-misha-voguel-7628484
40 www.pexels.com-misha-voguel-7628490
41 https://en.wikipedia.org/wiki/Dissociation_(psychology)
42 Van der Kolk, Bessel, MD, The Body Keeps the Score. Penguin Books, 2015.
43 Photos by cottonbro from Pexels
44 Image by Myriams-Fotos www.Pixabay.com
45 www.pexels.com by Robert Butts
46 pixabay.com by Maja Pejic
47 www.Pexels.com by cottonbro
48 www.Pexels.com by cottonbro

Thank you

Made in the USA
Columbia, SC
14 August 2024

b9b947b1-7e0d-415d-9559-6f43ef5aca4eR02